SELMA EVANS

TRAUMA
BONDING

Understanding & Breaking Free from the Emotional Chains That Keep Us Bound in Toxic Relationships

ISBN: 979-12-81498-02-0

TABLE OF CONTENTS

INTRODUCTION

Trauma is defined as "an event that causes profound psychological injury and suffering." The trauma bond is when a person bonds with an abuser for relief from their victimization. It becomes a toxic relationship where the victim will do anything to prevent their abuser from hurting them again. It makes the victim feel safer, loved, and reassured; it makes them feel like they are being cared for after all they have been through.

However, this toxic relationship creates a cycle of abuse that fuels further resentment and fear in the victim, ultimately creating more resentment. Acknowledging, recognizing, and breaking these bonds is extremely difficult for victims to do. Ultimately, however, it will lead to the healing of both the victim and their abuser if possible.

Trauma is often associated with the mind, but it is also intrinsically tied to the body. Often, the abuse creates permanent physical damage in the recipient. All too often, when a victim feels they cannot report their abuser for whatever reason, the prospect of surviving a trauma bond can become even more threatening than the actual attack itself.

Abusers often know this about victims and use it against them by threatening to kill their family or themselves if they dare to leave. This can create a vicious cycle of violence, leaving the victim with a sense of helplessness and hopelessness. This enables the abuser to control another human being and feed off their emotions. They will use this bond to continue perpetuating the cycle of abuse. This abuse may be physical, emotional, or sexual.

Once the victim can no longer take it, they start to withdraw or cut off contact with their friends and family. They are then left alone in a world where they are isolated from everyone except their abuser.

Fear and love are the biggest motivating factors that keep victims connected to their abusers.

PART 1 -
THE PROCESS
OF ESTABLISHING
TRAUMA BONDS

CHAPTER 1: MECHANISMS OF TRAUMA BONDING

Trauma bonding is comparable to Stockholm Syndrome, a condition in which individuals who have been kidnapped and held against their will develop feelings of trust or even affection for those who kidnapped and held them. In a relationship, this type of survival strategy can also be used. When a person is in a relationship with a narcissist or other abusive personality, a phenomenon known as trauma bonding can occur. In this situation, the abuser has overtaken the person's mind, rendering them unable to think rationally or make sound decisions or judgments.

One common symptom observed in both victims of Stockholm Syndrome and trauma bonding is the person's strong desire to remain in the situation or relationship. This may be in part because both victims are likely to be fearful or suspicious of any other adult figures who enter their lives.

The main difference between Stockholm Syndrome and trauma bonding is that the former involves an abduction wherein the victim is initially fearful of their captor, whereas the latter pertains to a relationship wherein the victim is actively protective of their abuser. The psychology behind Stockholm Syndrome and trauma bonding are similar, but they differ in their manifestation and expression.

Trauma bonding can occur in any traumatizing relationship, whether it is a long-lasting relationship or a brief one. There are, however, certain factors that make a person more susceptible to trauma bonding.

The narcissist's partner often has codependency issues and feels loved and cared for first in a trauma bond. However, over time, this begins to erode, and the relationship becomes dominated by emotional, mental, and sometimes physical abuse.

The codependent recognizes the change, but not why it is taking place. They believe that all that is required now is for them to ascertain what they are doing incorrectly in order to reintroduce the relationship's loving side.

If they break free, the narcissist only needs to return to the courtship phase to reclaim them. The trauma bond is strengthened as the codependent reaches out to the narcissist for love, recognition, and approval. This also means that if the abuse escalates, the codependent will stay in the relationship, perpetuating the destructive cycle.

Trauma bonding is defined as a person's devotion to a destructive person. Cycles of abuse and intermittent reward create a strong emotional bond between the victim and the perpetrator.

When an unhealthy bond is formed, it can be extremely difficult to break free. It can leave individuals feeling confused, powerless, and immobilized.

Contrary to common belief, a trauma bond does not require physical contact, such as sexual abuse or physical violence. It can include emotional abuse and verbal abuse – this includes yelling, name-calling, threatening, and cyberbullying. The abuser's words may feel like an attack and can leave the victim feeling helpless, causing intense fear and anxiety.

The victim's attachment to the perpetrator is rooted in survival tactics. After an abusive event, the victim may feel fearful and anxious and believe that the perpetrator is serious about their threats. The victim may feel obligated to obey any request or demand that the abuser makes, such as sending them a text message, speaking with them on the phone, or talking to them in person. The fear of loss of a relationship can be so strong that it forces the victim to avoid disapproval from their abuser.

The abuse cycle is a repetitive pattern, and can include physical, sexual, or emotional abuse; sometimes it consists of a combination of two or more types at once. However, the abuser is not only the perpetrator of the abuse, they are also the source of comfort and reward. Abusers behave in ways that confuse the victim. In some instances, the abuser may appear to love their partner, while in reality, they use their partner as a source of emotional energy or to fulfill their own needs. This can leave victims feeling alone and desperate for emotional support from their abuser.

What Makes a Relationship Traumatic?

The cycle of abuse and reward is what makes a relationship traumatic. A past or current unhealthy relationship can lead to trauma bonding. The victim continues to seek out the abuser and even pursues their affection because of the strong emotional investment. Consider the case of a person who has been physically abused by their spouse for years. This individual may believe there is no way out of the relationship because the abuser has told them that no one else can take care of them as well as they do.

Victims are then 'stuck in an emotional triangle,' which consists of three points:

1. The Victim

2. The Perpetrator

3. The Abusive Relationship

This triangle is a closed system that acts as a mechanism of post-traumatic growth. It functions in a self-regulating way that keeps the relationship intact and prevents the victim from leaving. Many people trapped in these abusive relationships believe that their abusive partners will change, and they find themselves unable to leave due to their fear of being abandoned. This can lead to confusion and helplessness as the victim does not know what to do next to end the abuse.

The triangle formation is a traumatic bond, which means there has been some trauma or fear imprinted in the relationship. As a result, the victim begins to believe that they are being mistreated, but they may feel that the abuse is the result of their own 'bad' behavior. These beliefs can lead victims to think that if they were smarter, prettier, or more successful, their abuser would stop abusing them. This then leads to feelings of worthlessness, self-hatred, and low self-worth. The abuser's emotional and verbal abuse may also be linked to the victim's low self-worth. It may be more difficult for the victim to leave their abusive relationship as a result of this.

Self-worth is a concept that stems from one's perception of their value. The assessment of self-worth is based on a person's sense of achievement, competence, independence, and self-esteem.

Low self-worth is defined as the perception of oneself as unlovable, inferior, or unworthy. This can lead to low self-esteem and an inability to trust others, causing the victim to withdraw from society to avoid the pain of rejection. The victim may also avoid negative feelings or events that could bring up their low self-worth and instead focus on other positive aspects of their life. This can lead them to stay in abusive relationships.

Trauma bonding occurs when a victim feels that they need a certain person in their life in order to be safe and feel secure. They may perceive their partner as the only thing standing between them and danger.

Perception of control is also a factor in trauma bonding. Victims may feel that their partner is watching everything they do and believe that they cannot spend time with friends or family without being controlled by their partner.

Frequency is another factor of trauma bonding. The frequency of abuse makes it difficult for victims to see an end to the cycle or relationship because they have become accustomed to frequent abuse.

Lack of knowledge about the cycle is another factor. Victims may not know what to do to break the cycle and may believe that nothing can be done because their abuser has said there will always be problems in their relationships. Victims, therefore, stay in abusive relationships because they fear being be left on their own with no support from their partner or family.

Trauma bonding can cause many different symptoms in a victim. It manifests itself through fear and panic, which makes it very difficult to leave the relationship.

The connection between the victim and their abusive partner can be very strong. This is due to the victim's inability to detach themselves from their abuser. They may believe that their abuser does not mean to hurt them – this is how a traumatizing relationship generally works. The abuser intimidates and scares the victim but then gives reassurance and love in order to keep the victim attached.

What are the Physical and Psychological Aspects of Trauma Bonding?

The mind and body react to trauma in two ways.

Physical Responses

Increased Heart Rate

SNS (sympathetic nervous system) stimulation is activated when we are in a fight or flight situation. It is characterized by tension, anxiety, and restlessness.

Poor Sleep Patterns

Sleep helps the body and mind calm down, but this is not possible when you are being abused. Sleeping problems include trouble falling or staying asleep, nightmares, and night terrors.

Difficulty Concentrating

When you are in fight or flight mode, your body places a higher premium on survival than on schoolwork or work projects.

Tension Headaches

Many people with trauma bonds experience headaches due to their elevated stress levels and their body's chemicals.

Abdominal Pain

During the fight or flight response, chemicals are released that causes blood to rush to vital organs like the liver, heart, and kidneys, often causing abdominal pain.

Increased Appetite

The body uses glucose and glycogen for energy, so it reserves the stored nutrients for survival.

Other Health Issues

Many individuals with trauma bonds experience various health problems such as stomach ulcers, headaches, or anxiety disorders. The body's immune system is often weakened, increasing the risk of developing a serious medical condition such as diabetes, heart disease, or cancer.

Psychological Responses

Depression

Trauma victims often feel constantly overwhelmed with fear and despair. They may experience depression, anxiety, or post-traumatic stress disorder.

Relationship Problems

Many victims don't have the energy to care for themselves. They may feel like they no longer have a connection with anyone other than their abusive partner. Sometimes this feeling of isolation leads to feelings of hopelessness and suicidal thoughts.

Self-Harm

Some victims use drugs or alcohol to cope with their feelings. They may also hurt themselves in other ways, such as cutting or burning.

Suicidal Thoughts and Behaviors

Some individuals with trauma bonds may feel worthless, hopeless, and helpless. Some people attempt suicide because they feel trapped.

Anxiety Disorders

Victims experience many irrational fears, such as fear for certain people, places, or things.

Low Self-Esteem

The constant criticism and blaming leaves victims feeling "bad" or "unlovable." They learn to see the abuse as their fault and then suffer from self-hatred or shame. Individuals with trauma bonds often believe they are not worthy of affection.

Trauma bonding is a process of attachment based on the victim's intense fear, dependence, and isolation. It does not mean that the victim is weak or stupid for staying in an unhealthy relationship – trauma bonding is a survival tactic caused by a traumatic experience.

Some research indicates that abuse victims may have certain personality characteristics that make them more susceptible to trauma bonding:

- *High levels of empathy* - This means the victim may feel a strong connection to others. They may be too trusting or helpful towards their abusive partner.

- *High levels of introversion* - Introverts are more prone to being involved in unhealthy relationships because they tend to suppress their feelings and thoughts about the abuse.

- *High levels of insecurity* - The victim may experience low self-esteem and develop a pattern of relying on other people for love and reassurance.

- *High levels of anxiety* - The victim may experience high stress levels from living with the fear of being abused and considering leaving the relationship

When you are being abused, you have to make sure that you have a support network of people who care about you. If no one loves you and cares about your well-being, it is normal to feel frustrated and depressed. Unfortunately, some people don't think that abuse is a problem or may not believe victims of violence. In this case, it is important to find a therapist who understands what abuse is and can provide support without blaming or criticizing the victim.

Trauma bonding is not a disorder but a reaction to being abused. People who have this trauma bond will likely experience symptoms of post-traumatic stress disorder (PTSD). Individuals that experience PTSD usually:

1. Re-experience Symptoms

These trauma symptoms include recurring memories of the event and feeling as if the trauma is being experienced over again.

This can occur in various ways, including flashbacks, night-mares, or frightening thoughts.

2. Avoid Stimuli

The victim may try to avoid life experiences, places, people, or feelings that make them feel like they are re-experiencing the trauma. They may even try to put up emotional barriers between themselves and other people, so they will be less likely to experience the symptoms associated with PTSD.

3. Experience Hyperarousal

This is when a person's nervous system is on high alert at all times, even during "normal" situations. This can result in the person being easily startled, anxious and tense.

4. Experience Negative Rumination

When negative thoughts occur, they are repeated over and over in one's mind.

5. Dissociate

This is when a person feels detached from their body and watches themselves from a distance.

6. Suffer Cognitive Avoidance

This is when a person avoids situations that potentially evoke or trigger the traumatic event(s) or the symptoms of PTSD.

7. Experience Positive Rumination

This is when a person discusses how to avoid re-experiencing the trauma or the symptoms of PTSD.

8. Are Hypervigilant

This is when a person is always paying attention to their environment, looking for danger at all times.

9. Have an Exaggerated Startled Response

This is when a person has a sudden feeling of fear or nervousness in response to an event that would not normally make a person react this way. This exaggeration of the normal startled response can be seen in combat veterans and victims of trauma bonding. It has been suggested that the exaggerated startled response might be responsible for victims not escaping from their abuser.

Victims of trauma bonding need to find someone who can understand their problems without blaming them or being judgmental. They may also seek professional counseling. Finally, victims should look for ways to improve their relationships with others and practice self-care techniques.

CHAPTER 2: WHEN DOES TRAUMATIC BONDING OCCUR?

T rauma bonding can happen when one is abused, threatened, or neglected. The traumatic event can range from an assault to a relationship break-up, but it has to be emotionally damaging for the victim.

The victim has to depend on the abuser for regular food, shelter, and money. This dependency can happen over time and can bring about trauma bonding.

The victim is often isolated from their friends and family. This isolation can restrict the victim's access to resources to help them get out of their situation.

Trauma Bonds Within a Family

A victim's personality and upbringing influence their recovery from trauma bonding. The victim will be more likely to sustain trauma bonding if they have been raised in one of these environments:

A Very Restrictive Home

Children who come from a home where they are not allowed free time or activities outside the house are more likely to develop trauma bonding. This includes homes and families that have religious beliefs that limit children's activities. In these cases, the children will likely not go to school or socialize with other children.

Abusive Parents

Childhoods with physically or emotionally abusive and neglectful parents can lead to trauma bonding. A child who is raised by an abusive parent must rely on that parent for food, shelter, and financial support. The victim of trauma bonding might be left alone in their room for hours or even days during their abuse. This is not only a problem of survival but can impact their physical health and mental well-being.

An Emotionally Neglectful Family

This is when a child is not treated well by the adults in their life. These kids can be the victims of physical, emotional, or sexual abuse, but not necessarily all simultaneously. They might also be neglected in the sense of being left alone for long periods, not getting fed or showered, or being ignored by their parents when they tell them about a problem.

Trauma Bonds between Romantic Partners

Trauma bonding can happen when two people are in an intimate relationship. Some situations that can lead to trauma bonding are:

Family of Origin

The victim might have been verbally or physically abused by their mother, father, or other family members while growing up. They may have been told they were not worth anything, and that no one wanted them around.

Isolation

Trauma bonding is more likely to happen when a victim is isolated from their friends and family. The isolation prevents the victim from seeking other relationships outside of the one they have with the abuser. Often this isolation also involves manipulation on behalf of the abuser, who may make up excuses for why their spouse needs time alone or away from others.

A Fearful and Manipulative Partner

The victim may be afraid of their partner or in a situation where they need to follow orders. They cannot make decisions for themselves, which puts them in a position where they have no power. Victims who have been cut off from friends, family, and normal relationships are more likely to believe that they do not deserve better treatment.

Trauma Bonding through Sexual Abuse

Sexual abuse can happen during marriage, dating, or even during childhood. Anyone, regardless of gender, ethnicity, or race, can be sexually abused. Rape is a type of sexual abuse that occurs in many relationships. It is the abuse of power in which a person uses their body to cause harm to another person. Abuse can also occur when one partner demands a sexual act that their partner does not want to do.

In domestic violence situations where there is sexual abuse, it is often about power and control. Abusers will continue to force their victims into having sex until they know they have no other choice but to cooperate with them for survival purposes.

There are three types of relationships in the context of trauma bonding:

The Rescuer-Victim Relationship

A rescuer is someone who uses their good looks, charm or other means to help a "needy" person. They feel that they deserve special treatment from this person and might abuse them. The victim might develop a feeling of gratitude towards their abuser and go back to them over and over again. Even if the victim manages to leave the relationship, they may go back if the abuser asks for another chance.

The Victim-Abuser Relationship

It is when a victim believes that they deserve to be treated badly and gives up on fighting against their abuse. They might also feel as if they were responsible for their abuse because of something they did or said, so they become accustomed to it.

The Abuser-Abuser Relationship

In this case, two people abused each other growing up. This shows how the abuse cycle can complicate family relationships and can lead to trauma bonding between family members.

Trauma Bonds Between Peers

Trauma bonding can also happen in peer relationships. The victim can also suffer from secondary traumatic stress if their social group does not support them. This could be happening because they have been bullied or because the group does not understand their trauma.

There are many different ways that trauma bonding can happen between peers:

- The bystanders might be afraid to get involved with the bullying. So, they ignore what is going on to protect themselves from being hurt by the bully or the bully's friends. Some kids will walk away from the scene of a fight and pretend it did not happen.

- There are times when witnesses of bullying will not know how to help a victim, so they do nothing at all or start laughing at them as if it was funny for someone else to be hurt. This can happen at school or in the neighborhood.

- Some kids may say that there is nothing they can do. Sometimes, bystanders of bullying may also laugh about it.

If a victim has been bullied before, they may not want to tell anyone what is happening or ask for help. They might even be afraid to make new friends because they have lost the ability to trust people.

Below are a few terms used to describe elements of trauma bonding:

Circling

In this situation, one child begins to bully the other at school or home. The victim may keep their feelings a secret, hoping that the bully will stop. They may even believe it is their responsibility to be nice to their abuser or bully. The bully might tell the victim not to tell anyone about what has happened.

Fleeing

To flee is similar to running away from bullies or leaving school for any reason. The victims of bullying might get scared and run away because they are afraid of being bullied or made fun of again.

Ganging Up

The bully is likely to get stronger as more kids join their gang, so the victim becomes less likely to do something about it.

Trauma Reenactment

This happens when the victim begins to repeat what has happened to them as if they were trying to stop it from happening again. The victim may bully someone else because they want to change their role in the situation.

The Chemistry of Trauma Bonding

The abuser uses charm, persuasion, and power to get what they want out of their relationship. They also pressure their victims into doing things they don't want to do and might have co-dependency that leads them to stay with this kind of person. Trauma bonding can lead to a strong chemical relationship between two people, which can be dangerous because it keeps them together even when they do not get along.

The Release of Oxytocin and Cortisol

Oxytocin, commonly called the "cuddle hormone," is a chemical that people release when they are in love or have feelings of tenderness toward another person. It makes people feel close and connected both physically and emotionally. The opposite of this chemical is the stress hormone cortisol, which people release when they are in situations that make them feel threatened, overwhelmed, or anxious. This can cause them to fall into old patterns of trauma bonding because their body tells them to stay away from the danger, in the same way that their body would do before the trauma bonding occurred in their life.

Cortisol can also be released when an abusive person has a flashback to a traumatic event. Even after healing from the trauma, it can be difficult for a victim to leave their abuser because their body reacts in the same way it did when they were still being abused. This can happen after a victim has left and come back several times, each time getting more attached and having more of an emotional reaction to staying in the abusive relationship because of how their bodily reaction.

The following are some examples of trauma bonding in books and TV shows:

- **J.K. Rowling's *Harry Potter* series** - The main character is a wizard whose uncle and aunt abuse him because they think he is a freak. As time goes on, Harry gets used to being abused because he has spent so much time at home with his aunt and uncle. He does not want to be around them anymore but does not know where to go or who can help him get away from them.

- ***The Lord of the Flies* by William Golding** is a famous story of victims being stranded on an island. The main character, Ralph, becomes the leader because he tries to take control and care for the kids by pretending that everything is okay. When a boy named Jack starts to try and take control of him, Ralph gets jealous and wants to stop him from taking any more power than he already has.

- ***Song of Solomon*** - Toni Morrison's book is about a man named Milkman who is searching for his identity in life. He gets stuck in relationships with women that abuse him and leave him feeling powerless. He is a confused boy who feels like he can't get out of the trauma bond with his abuser.

Trauma bonding is an important topic for women's studies. It can be used as an example of how women are often taught to think and act by society. Women may be taught to stay in bad relationships or situations that they know are not good for them or their family, thus they tend not to leave abusive relationships even if they want to.

CHAPTER 3: TRAUMA BONDING IN RELATIONSHIPS

A trauma bond can be especially prevalent in romantic relationships due to the private and personal nature that intimacy typically brings. The consequences can be devastating.

Emotional and Psychological Abuse

Emotional or psychological trauma can be particularly difficult to identify, although they can be just as damaging as sexual or physical trauma. Emotional abuse is often not discussed with the same frequency as physical abuse, but it puts an individual at a high risk of developing a trauma bond with their abuser. Emotional abuse causes detrimental effects to the emotions and behaviors of an individual. People who have been emotionally abused may feel resentment, fear, helplessness, anxiety, loneliness, and depression. Psychological abuse can include verbal attacks on an individual's personality or character, behavior modification tactics, and threats that cause a victim to feel afraid for their safety. These symptoms can be difficult to process because of their hidden and covert nature. Because of this, victims of emotional abuse must receive psychological and emotional support to help them understand how their abuser has affected them.

Physical and Sexual Abuse

Physical and sexual abuse in intimate relationships has been a widespread problem, especially in past generations. These types of abuse are defined as violent acts that cause physical harm to a victim. Abuse can include pushing, shoving, hitting, kicking, or punching; throwing objects; strangling or choking; burning or scalding with hot water; driving recklessly with a partner in the car; forced sex or sexual touching without consent; kidnapping; and torture. Physical abuse also includes threats of violence, including brandishing a gun to control a partner's behavior through fear.

Physical abuse is intentional and the result of coercive tactics from the abuser. It can be difficult to spot an abusive partner early on. Someone who has been physically abused is at a high risk of developing a trauma bond with their abuser. They may feel they are responsible for their partner's behavior, feel they deserve it and that nothing better will come along, and/or try to make sense of the abuse by justifying it as minor or acceptable. In addition, victims are often ashamed that they were in a relationship with someone who would hurt them, so they may not seek help from others to keep their secrets safe.

Sexual abuse can be perpetrated against both men and women and can include acts of force, such as rape, unwanted sexual touching or kissing and sexual advances without consent.

Sexual abuse is often a difficult topic to discuss, and victims are often afraid that they will be blamed if they tell others about the abuse. In addition, many victims experience shame and embarrassment. Women account for the majority of victims, although young girls and boys (ages 12–17) are also particularly vulnerable to sexual abuse.

Financial Abuse

Because it is not physically visible and has no immediate consequences, financial abuse is frequently overlooked. This happens when one partner or family member uses financial information to gain or maintain financial dominance and influence over their partner or family members. The financial abuser may be the partner or caregiver in the relationship, but it could also be a family member of either the victim or abuser. Financial abuse often occurs after a victim has experienced another type of violence or controlling behavior in the relationship. Financial abuse is also a component of emotional and psychological abuse.

Financial abuse may be easier to spot than other forms of domestic violence because there are some distinguishing characteristics that can help someone recognize if they or someone they know is being abused financially. The abuser may have complete control over their partner's financial resources, including their paychecks and bank accounts, as well as the ability to use credit cards and other forms of credit in their name without their consent. When one partner, usually the abuser, is in total control of the household finances, it can be challenging for a victim to access the money they need for expenses such as rent or groceries. Specifically targeting someone for financial gain is another factor that indicates financial abuse; in a healthy relationship, both partners tend to benefit from any shared purchases and earnings.

Financial abuse frequently occurs in conjunction with other forms of domestic violence and extends beyond a single act of greed. Financial abuse can include preventing a partner from working or getting an education because it could mean more money or better opportunities outside of the home. It can also include pulling a partner out of school, or giving verbal or physical threats to prevent them from going to work.

Gaslighting

Gaslighting is a form of psychological abuse in which one person attempts to convince the other that what they are experiencing is not true. Gaslighting can be an emotional abuse tactic used by one partner, parents or caregivers to young children, or adults with disabilities. This practice can also be used in groups, such as families and churches, to manipulate others into believing their experiences are unreal. Gaslighting can also manipulate someone's behavior through degradation, guilt, intimidation, and control.

Gaslighting is most often done slowly so the abuser can break down their victim's sense of self-worth and make them more dependent on the abuser. Gaslighting causes a person to question what they know is true. The primary goal of gaslighting is to cause the victim to distrust themselves and their perception of reality. Once this is achieved, the victim becomes more dependent on the abuser.

A parent or caregiver may also use gaslighting in an attempt to make a young child believe that their experiences are not real, such as when they have abused the child. In this situation, the abuser may use gaslighting to gain control over the child's behavior and choices because it lessens their ability to trust in themselves and their own ability to determine their own needs, boundaries, and limits.

The Rescuer Complex

The rescuer complex is a psychological control used by a person who controls a vulnerable partner. The abuser may have initially used emotional abuse, neglect, or physical abuse to isolate the victim. In the rescuer complex, the abuser becomes responsible for taking care of the victim. This behavior may include making medical decisions for the victim without their consent or refusing to allow their partner to seek medical treatment when it is needed. Abusers may even argue with medical providers about whether or not an individual needs care to ensure that they do not miss out on additional punishment from an abusive relationship.

Parenting/Caretaking

Parenting and caretaking in abusive relationships are common scenarios. Abuse victims may be emotionally, physically, and sexually abused by someone they depend on for support, including their parent, other relative or family friend, or a partner. When the abused person is a child, it can be even more challenging because they cannot be as vocal about their abuse and may lack the ability to advocate or protect themselves from further harm.

Some abusers may have one or more children and care for them within an abusive relationship. This type of relationship is often called "caretaking" or "parenting by proxy." This type of abuse is a common occurrence in high-conflict and narcissistic relationships. An abuser may believe that they own their children and want to control who they live with, what they do, how they spend their time, and whom they associate with. Abuse of this nature can last for years, if not generations.

Abusers may also use their children to gain attention by making false accusations against their partner and using the courts to gain custody of the children so that they can continue controlling their partner through manipulation and isolation.

This type of control is also used in many parental abduction cases when a custodial parent gains primary custody after making false accusations against the noncustodial parent, who then has fewer rights and visitation access with their children. Custodial parents may impose rules on the noncustodial parent by dictating how they can see their children or telling them where to pick up and drop off their children for visitation; if an abuser does not follow these rules, they may use this as an excuse to gain full custody.

After the Abuse

In the aftermath of their abuse, victims often have a hard time trusting themselves and knowing what they should do. They may begin to question whether or not they deserved the abuse they received.

A victim may also have trouble trusting other people in relationships because they feel like everyone will abandon them or treat them poorly. This can lead to social anxiety and difficulty building new relationships. They often are afraid of intimacy and push people away before they can be abandoned again.

Victims of emotional, physical, sexual, financial, and psychological abuse often do not want to be in another relationship because they fear being hurt again. A victim may not want to date or be close with anyone because they are afraid it will trigger memories of their past abuse.

CHAPTER 4:
THE PROCESS OF DEVELOPING TRAUMA BONDS: A SEVEN-STAGE JOURNEY

The majority of people can break the toxic bonds of an abusive relationship. However, some individuals cannot do so, and their mental health is severely compromised. They experience severe anxiety or depression and have difficulty forming trusting relationships. What makes the difference? How can we understand why some people have difficulty freeing themselves from the toxic bonds of an abusive relationship?

Firstly, it is helpful to understand how trauma bonds are formed. Here are the seven stages:

1. Love Bombing

This is a form of manipulative behavior that an abusive partner uses to create intense emotions in their partner. Often, it is done right after the controlling partner has been abusive. The abuser will engage in excessive attention and communication with their significant other, such as having flowers delivered to them at work, spending entire evenings on the phone with them, or complimenting them excessively. This keeps the abused partner from leaving. This period usually lasts for about three weeks. During this time, the abusive partner will attempt to manipulate the victim into thinking that they have control over their actions by behaving charmingly and looking as attractive as possible. Love bombing may make the victim feel guilty for wanting to leave, and this guilt may cause them to stay in the relationship longer than they would otherwise. If the victim leaves the relationship, they may be further manipulated into believing that their own actions led to breakdown of the relationship, and that when they come back, all will be forgiven.

2. Trust and Dependency

The abuser will use trust and dependency to involve the victim in their life completely. The abuser may spend a great deal of time on the phone talking to their partner, giving them advice, or creating a feeling that they can rely on the abuser's choices. This behavior is used to keep the victim in the relationship and make them feel as though they cannot survive without their abuser. They may feel as though they have no one but the abuser to trust, which makes it more likely that they will stay in the relationship regardless of how they feel.

As trust and dependency are created, the victim will start to believe that their abuser needs them as much as they need their abuser. This will often lead to the victim putting the abuser's needs before their own.

3. Devaluing

The abuser will often make their partner feel as if they are worthless or a waste of time through belittling, yelling, or insults. The abuser may also fail to recognize their partner's achievements and gifts, which causes them to feel inadequate and unimportant. This behavior is used when the abuser wants to cause the victim pain or humiliation rather than solve a problem or resolve an issue. This can take the form of yelling in front of their friends or family, insulting them in front of others, withdrawing from them, or making them feel like they don't matter.

De-valuing is used to make the victim feel as though they have no control over their actions and that if they leave, they will have no one to love them or even care for them because they are so worthless. This behavior causes the victim to stay with their abuser. Because their self-esteem may be so low, the victim may not have the confidence to leave, and they may believe that they do not deserve their own life away from the abuser.

4. Manipulation/Gaslighting

It is common for an abuser to start manipulating their partner by making them think that they are the one with the problem. Gaslighting is a psychological trick in which the abuser convinces the victim that something false occurred. This can make the victim feel like they did something to upset their abuser or cause them to feel bad about themselves for another reason.

Gaslighting causes the victim to doubt themselves, making them question their decisions and feelings. The abuser will make up events or lie to make it seem like the victim did something bad, further hurting their self-esteem and self-worth. This behavior is also used to make the victim feel that they are to blame for their partner's abusive actions. This causes them to feel like a burden and less worthy than others.

Suppose a victim believes that they are at fault for what happened in their relationship. In this case, it can be very difficult for them to break away from an abusive relationship because of how much shame and guilt the gaslighting has caused them to feel. Even if a victim does leave an abusive relationship, their guilt can make it even more difficult for them to move on. This causes many victims to become dependent on their abuser for their emotional well-being and self-worth.

Because the abuser does not want their spouse to go, he or she may employ deception to keep the victim from leaving. If a victim does leave, the abuser will then use gaslighting to make them feel they were at fault for what happened when they were abused, making it even harder for them to move on.

5. Giving Up Control

The abuser may do things for their partner, such as paying the bills or cleaning up their mess. This manipulation can be used to make the victim feel as though they have to return the favor.

The abuser may hold a lot of control over their partner, including when they leave or what they do. This keeps the victim from leaving and having any freedoms.

The behavior has been described as a form of emotional abuse (coercive control). It has been studied as a form of domestic violence in which the victim may stay with their abuser even though, physically, they can leave. It causes feelings of powerlessness and worthlessness and can hurt the victim's self-esteem.

The abuser may also make the victim feel there is nowhere for them to go if they leave. This keeps the victim dependent on their abuser. The victim may also be fearful of leaving their abuser if they are told something bad will happen to them or their children. It is often easier for these victims to stay in an abusive relationship than to leave and make such drastic changes in their lives.

6. Losing Yourself

The abuser may make the victim feel like there is no one else in the world and that they are all alone, with no friends, family, or money to support themselves. This type of abuse makes the victim believe that their abuser is the only person who cares about them. As a result, the victim may use self-harming behaviors, such as cutting themselves and burning themselves with cigarettes. Even though the victim wants to leave, a part of them does not want to because they are afraid of what will happen without their abuser. They feel as if they have nowhere else to go and do not have any friends. They may also feel that they cannot take care of themselves or anyone else. The abuser will do anything to make their victim believe that they cannot make it without them.

7. Addiction to the Cycle

Often, the abuser does not think of their actions as abuse. They may use any tactic available to them, including charm, manipulation, or physical force, to control their victims. If the victim leaves, the abuser will soon become uncomfortable and try their best to get them back with apologies or anything else they can offer. The victim may feel the abuser needs them, and they will stay even though they are being abused.

A victim of abuse may stay in the relationship for many years and continue to be abused, despite their constant thoughts about leaving. They may have a hard time leaving their abuser because of their dependence on them. They will feel like they are nothing or no one without their abuser and will not want to leave the relationship until the situation worsens. This is called a vicious cycle. The abuser will try anything to get them back, like making excuses for their behavior, blaming others for what they do, and offering gifts or anything else that makes them feel better. The abuser will also threaten their victims to keep them in the relationship. This keeps the victim unsure of what their life will be like if they leave and makes it harder for them to get out of the situation. Because they have been trapped in the cycle for so long, they are likely to make excuses or try to convince themselves that the abuser does care about them.

CHAPTER 5: STRATEGIES AND EXERCISES TO BREAK TRAUMA BONDS

S ome exercises and tools can be used to break trauma bonds in relationships.

The dissolution of trauma bonds often begins with the victim distancing themselves from their abuser. However, this step can be difficult as the abuser will often react with more anger and denial; thus, it becomes necessary to keep distancing oneself despite the increasing hostility of the abuser.

An important step is to find support from healthy relationships. Ask for help from a friend, family member, or counselor, and make an effort to develop real friendships whenever possible.

It is also important not to become too involved in the thoughts of the abuser; we mustn't dwell on negative outcomes such as being alone or gaining the attention of others through gossip. These things are driven by self-pity and sympathy, so avoiding them is a good idea.

Treating oneself with self-respect and dignity helps immensely. It is also crucial that we are comfortable with ourselves and do not feel obligated to remain in abusive relationships because our core values have been threatened.

Another way of breaking a trauma bond is through cognitive behavioral therapy (CBT) and identifying the effect of the trauma bond. CBT can help you see how your fear, shame, blame, and responsibility manifests in everyday life and influences your thoughts and behavior.

A crucial step in breaking a trauma bond is acknowledging, recognizing, and accepting that we have been abused and it is not our fault.

By expressing anger or distancing and remaining emotionally disengaged from the abuser, one can break the trauma bond by creating a sense of closure and achieving a system of healthy boundaries.

When small steps are taken to break a trauma bond, this can be the beginning of long-term healing.

Hypnosis for Trauma

Some many techniques and therapies can be used to help victims of trauma. One of these techniques is hypnosis. Hypnosis is a state where an individual's awareness is heightened by suggestion or relaxation. This can be used to break the cycle of abuse in relationships. The reason hypnosis works so well for traumatized victims is because of a reprogramming process called neuro-association that occurs during hypnosis. In this process, the subject learns how to associate positive thoughts with their abuser and re-integrate traumatic memories into their conscious mind until their abuser's actions or words no longer trigger them. This can become a tool that trauma victims can use to counteract the painful effects of abuse and trauma.

In the right person's hands, hypnosis can be a safe and effective method to help those unable to overcome their traumatic memories. It is important to note that hypnosis is only one form of therapy and should not replace traditional talk therapy. It is often believed that by using hypnosis, someone will become instantly cured; this is incorrect, although many victims have found success through this method.

Talk Therapy

Talk therapy is one of the most common types of therapy used to help victims who have endured traumatic experiences. The victim is encouraged to talk about their experiences, ask questions, and find out what they may have missed in their journey to recovery. It is crucial that victims keep notes or a journal with them so they can write down anything they need to while they are undergoing treatment. This helps them stay focused, and writing down their feelings and emotions may lead them to have breakthroughs in their recovery process.

Cognitive Behavioral Therapy

As touched on above, another method that can be useful for victims of trauma is cognitive behavioral therapy. In this method, the victim is encouraged to recognize the negative ways they may have thought or reacted in their lives and work towards changing these behaviors. This process may help a victim realize that they are making decisions based upon their past experiences and may be acting out of fear or influenced by their abuser. Acknowledging these things and changing behavior can lead them to make better decisions in the future. This teaches victims that they can change themselves and make better choices in the future, making them more psychologically healthy.

Eye Movement Desensitization Reprocessing (EMDR)

Another therapy that can be used in helping victims of trauma is eye movement desensitization reprocessing (EMDR). In this method, the victim is encouraged to relive their traumatic memories with the help of a therapist. EMDR therapy works so well for abuse victims because it helps them become more aware of their history, understand why they reacted or behaved in certain ways, and differentiate themselves from their abuser through positive healing activities. A major aspect of EMDR therapy is that it teaches victims to use positive coping skills to help overcome their traumatic experiences, develop better relationship skills, and learn how to identify potential abusers before entering into a relationship.

Cultivate Positive Moments

Some simple suggestions to overcome traumatic experiences are keeping a journal or "feelings" page, talking with friends and family members, and being patient with your recovery process.

It makes sense that trauma also has a lasting mental effect on an individual. Flashbacks of the trauma, nightmares, hyper-vigilance (watching everything very carefully), extreme stress reactions in similar situations, such as anxiety and panic attacks, depression, and so on, can all occur. All these symptoms are due to the secretion of cortisol by our adrenal glands. Therefore, an individual who suffers from trauma may also have low cortisol levels in the body.

The work of "traumatization" was initially developed by Robert J. Lifton to describe the effects of critical or near-death experiences on human beings that preceded or accompanied the experience. He also described how such experiences might affect individuals' lives afterwards, including their relationships with others, their values, and beliefs, their worldviews and opinions about themselves, their social position, their ability to connect with others, as well as their physical health.

Put your attention on the positive aspects of your life. List down the things you're grateful for today.

1

____

2

____

3

____

4

____

5

____

6

____

7

____

2. Writing down your goals every day can give you something to look forward to and work towards. This is also a good way to

remind yourself that you have things to look forward to in your future.

1

____

2

____

3

____

4

____

5

____

6

____

7

____

3. List the things you are looking forward to this week.

1

____

2

____

3

____

4

____

5

____

6

____

7

____

4. Make a shortlist of positive memories from your past.

1

____

2

____

3

____

4

5

Energy Healing

Energy healing can help remove the trauma caused by past events from the body while connecting to all of those traumatized cells deeper within the body. This is then used as a form of healing which connects with your inner child and heals your spirit. The practitioner uses guided imagery and energetic tools such as sound, color, and light work to help guide the victim into a place of peace within themselves that allows them to heal and forgive. This healing is not only helpful for the individual but also for all family members who have been affected by this trauma, allowing them to move forward in their lives.

Healing Trauma Through the Use of Sunlight

1. Lie down in natural sunlight with your arms and legs extended.

2. Breathe deeply and focus on relaxing.

3. You may want to imagine yourself as a light being and connect with the sun through that imagery. You may also find it helpful

to associate the light with something you are grateful for, such as "I am thankful for this light shining through me."

4. For one minute, focus on what you are thankful for, then allow yourself to relax and bask in the light of the sun for the next seven minutes.

5. During these seven minutes, focus on any area of your body that requires healing.

Healing Trauma Through the Use of Nature

1. Go to a place in nature that makes you feel at peace. This may be a park, beach, forest, or any place outside where you will not be distracted by other people's conversation or movement.

2. Sit comfortably and close your eyes; breathe deeply while still focusing on making this place feel peaceful.

3. Take a moment to imagine how you may felt at the time of your traumatic incident, and imagine a way in which you can heal this trauma.

4. Spend another five minutes, making sure you feel at peace in this area. If your mind wanders at all during this time, direct your attention back to this peaceful place and focus on what it feels like to remain calm and peaceful.

5. After five minutes, take a moment to stand up and scan the area around you for anything that might have been overlooked or forgotten during your session.

6. If any areas of your physical body need healing, take a moment to reflect upon them and imagine how you can release any negative emotions from them.

7. Repeat the exercise if needed.

Meditation

Meditation can be a useful tool to combat trauma bonding. This technique has been used by many to help release trauma stored in the body. The calming properties of meditation allow the patient to relax, cope with the past and heal.

Scientific studies have shown that meditation can break any trauma bond. Many of the patients in these studies have suffered from abuse, alcoholism, or other traumatic experiences; however, those who practice this technique find that it makes them feel more calm and relaxed and able to cope with issues from their past.

The most important aspect of meditation for breaking traumatic bonds is mindfulness meditation. During this type of meditation, you focus on the present moment and allow any conscious thoughts to flow freely. For example, if a memory from a traumatic event pops into your head, you accept it but do not give it power over you because if you allow it to go unchecked, it will continue to affect you. This technique allows patients to feel relaxed and safe in the present moment.

Through meditation, patients can release any negative thoughts associated with their trauma and let go of those memories that may be weighing them down. They can also imagine healing their body through meditation and connecting with spiritual energy they may not have otherwise connected with. Once they've made this connection, they can begin to heal themselves and those around them by understanding what happened during the event, feeling no guilt or shame, and letting go of the trauma they've been holding on to.

Here is how you can meditate to release a trauma bond

1. Find a quiet place where you will not be disturbed for 5 minutes.

2. Close your eyes and take deep breaths as you sit in a comfortable position.

3. Focus on your breathing and being in the moment, thinking about how you are feeling in this moment in time.

4. Think about what you want to focus on during this session of meditation: perhaps it is a memory or event that has caused you

pain in the past, maybe it was something that happened with another person, or maybe even something that happened with yourself – anything that is bothering you now that you would like to release it.

4. Go back to this thought and focus on it in a positive light, releasing any negative thoughts and feelings you have about it by imagining yourself being at peace with the memory.

5. Continue focusing on your breathing and the thought you are trying to release until you feel calm and relaxed.

6. Think of anything else that is bothering you right now, whether it be a memory or something else going on in your life. Repeat steps 3-5 until all of these negative memories are gone from your mind.

7. Finally, feel at peace and ready to return to the real world and your normal routine.

It is important to understand which part of the brain is responsible for the "turning off" during traumatic events to facilitate trauma release. Called the right hippocampus, this area plays a key role in enabling trauma victims to remember the past without being emotionally affected. After trauma, many individuals can recall the traumatic event while still feeling a sense of safety and control in their present situation. When this occurs, the trauma bond begins to diminish, and the victim can achieve a state of serenity.

Breaking the Relationship

Although it may be difficult to break the relationship between a victim and their abuser, there are ways you can make interactions with your abuser less traumatic.

What you can do:

1. Avoid sharing any trauma memories with your abuser and show that you don't want to revisit the past.

2. Keep your communication to a minimum as less contact with them may be better.

3. Do not take care of your abuser's needs and never turn to them for comfort or advice.

4. Be clear about your boundaries and expectations with your abuser, so you can protect yourself from further abuse and deal with the traumatic event in a healthy way.

5. Put as much distance between yourself and your abuser as you can so that you can feel at peace and are able to rebuild a new life for yourself.

6. Accept that you cannot control the abuser and do not feel responsible for their actions.

It is important to understand that serenity can only be fully achieved when the person stops thinking about their trauma bond(s). Looking after your physical and mental health is crucial at this time. Below are some important things to consider:

1. Medication - If your medication doesn't work anymore, talk to your doctor about switching to something else.

2. Therapy - Work with a therapist or counselor to deal with the issues caused by the traumatic experience.

3. Diet – Many people resort to comfort eating when they're upset or struggling with trauma. Check in with how you're feeling, and make an effort to eat a healthy diet.

4. Sleep cycle - Sleep is when your body heals itself from everything that's happened throughout your day. Ensure that you get at least 6–8 hours of sleep per night to help keep your mind clear and focused.

5. Exercise – Exercise is important for your body, mind, and soul. It's also a great way to combat depression or anxiety and make you feel better about yourself.

Finding the Core of Your Toxic Relationship

1. The first step is to recognize the effect the abuse has had on you. List at least two ways the abuse has affected you:

1

____

2

____

2. The difference between a healthy and unhealthy relationship is that healthy relationships are built on love, respect, trust, and other positive emotions. Unhealthy relationships are unhealthy because they involve abuse to control their partner. There are many ways to define abuse, but the main common theme is that an abuser tries to control their significant other by hurting them and making them feel worthless. Labeling the abuse – emotional or physical – is key to understanding that it is not normal or healthy for anyone to treat another person this way. List two specific abuser behaviors that have been directed at you.

1

____

2

____

Breaking a trauma bond is possible, but it will be difficult, as the abuse you suffered has likely deeply affected how you see yourself today. Taking these steps in the order listed may help with the process:

-

Set boundaries - Make clear decisions about what is acceptable to you and what is not. Make sure your loved ones are aware of your boundaries and will support them, whether or not they initially agree with you.

- Record your memories – Write down your memories of the events that happened to you and where you were when they happened so you can remember everything clearly.

- Realize that abuse is not normal - Ask yourself if you think what the abuser did is acceptable, and decide for yourself if it was or not.

- Talk to someone who can help - Talk to a friend, family member, or counselor about what happened so you can work through it together and better understand how to give yourself the support needed at this time.

- Remove anything that reminds you of the abuse - Remove objects, photos, gifts, and other memorabilia that remind you of what happened to you, so it does not keep dragging you back into that time and place. Letting go of the memory can be difficult, but it is important to move on from whatever actions have taken place to heal and take control over your life again.

- If you are currently trying to break the trauma bond,

but your loved ones have not responded healthily, recognize that you don't have to solve the problem with them. Respect their autonomy as individuals.

Sometimes, we detach from painful memories because we do not want to remember them or relive them. This can happen when the memories are too upsetting or painful for us to process and heal from them, especially if we avoid thinking about it and keep going on with our lives as if it did not happen. In this way, we are detached from our past and even from ourselves. This may happen because the memory of the event is too painful for us to process or because it may not seem real, even after having experienced it. The person who abused you will try to keep your relationship together because they want to keep their power over you.

PART 2 - IDENTIFYING A TRAUMA BOND

CHAPTER 6: 12 SIGNS OF TRAUMATIC BONDING

There are many signs that someone has a trauma bond. Sometimes the signs are subtle, however, as the relationship goes on, the victim will begin to experience confusion and despair, which will need to be acknowledged and addressed.

The main components of a trauma bond are:

- Cyclical nature - It can be difficult to break a trauma bond. The victim often feels powerless and helpless. Many will have difficulty understanding their feelings and experience numbness or detachment. They may also feel that the abuser is "all that exists" for them and begin to believe the abuse was their fault.

- Power imbalance - In a trauma bond, the abuser has

power or control over their partner. This is often because the abusive partner knows how to manipulate
their partner and cause them to feel as if they are to
blame for whatever is happening.

- Fear – In a trauma bond, the victim will be afraid of
the abuser. Often, this fear will make it difficult for the
victim to leave.

- Self-doubt – In a trauma bond, one may begin to
doubt themselves and their perceptions. This can often lead them to feel confused and helpless. A partner
may have difficulty trusting themselves and others.

- Dissociative tendencies - There may be a tendency to
avoid situations and people reminiscent of the abuse or
the victim may find it difficult to make decisions. They
may also feel guilt, shame, and regret.

- Self-blame - The partner may have thoughts of: "I
should have known better, done more, known what
was happening." This can lead to dissociation, where
there is a tendency to shut down emotionally and
become numb. The extreme form of dissociation is
self-mutilation.

- "Uncontrollability" - This occurs when the victim feels
they could not leave the relationship because they be-

lieved they would be killed if they did so.

- Self-harm - In a trauma bond, victims may begin to hurt themselves. They may believe that it will alleviate the pain and isolation they experience. Additionally, they may be motivated by a fear of losing control.

- Shame - In a trauma bond, one will often feel trapped by their partner. The victim may be ashamed of what is happening and will find it hard to escape due to guilt or shame.

- Isolation - Often, victims in trauma bonds will not have anyone to talk to about their feelings and distress. They may feel that their partner would abuse them even more if they did. This is because the partner has power over the individual seeking help.

- Minimal awareness - Many abuse victims will fail to recognize that they are in a trauma bond. They may be unaware that what is happening is abuse or may be brushed off as "being angry," "making an excuse," or "too sensitive." This means they are not aware of what is happening and will continue to tolerate it. It also means the partner may have no idea how severe the trauma bond actually is or how badly it affects them.

- Feeling Crazy - The abuser will usually control their

partner with jealousy and make them feel as though they are crazy. This leads the victim to become confused, anxious, and upset.

Behavioral Transformations

Victims in trauma bonds often change their behavior. They may:

- Become withdrawn - Victims can become isolated and lose interest in the world around them. They will begin to feel as though they are losing a part of themselves.

- Become depressed - When a partner is in a trauma bond, they will experience many emotions such as fear, anxiety, and anger. These will often lead to depression because they feel powerless and unable to cope with what is happening. This is not the "regular" type of depression where we feel sad or down for periods, but where you feel so powerless that it stops you from functioning normally.

- Have a sense of hopelessness - Many victims will feel as though there is no way they can ever escape the abuse they are suffering and will begin to accept their abuser's behavior. This results in being frozen into inaction and feeling that there is no point in dealing with the situation.

- Show early signs of an eating disorder - There is often a tendency for partners to seek approval from others when they have been abused. This can occur because of their need for control over their environment and themselves. Their abuser will often focus on looks or weight rather than other attributes, leading to the partner's desire to diet to please them.

- Suffer from insomnia or nightmares - For most people, sleep is something that helps restore us. When we are abused or feel we are being abused, it can be difficult to sleep as this helps us escape from our abuser. Sleepwalking and nightmares often occur when a victim has an altered consciousness due to anxiety, stress, or dissociation.

- Avoid eye contact - When a person is trapped in a trauma bond, they may avoid eye contact with their partner. This may occur because the victim feels their partner will judge them and do the exact opposite of what they want. It might also occur because the abuser is intimidating.

- Become less attentive - Partners in trauma bonds often become less attentive to each other and feel as if they are seeing or hearing things that are not there. This usually occurs because of loud noises or flashing lights when under stress. This can lead to suspicion and paranoia, resulting in the abuser gaining further control over their partner.

- Social isolation - One of the main effects of a trauma bond is a sense of shame when trying to tell others about their abuse. Individuals may withdraw from social activities, which will cause them to feel lonely and isolated once more.

- Drop out of hobbies or interests - Most people have a hobby or interest that involves interacting with other people, which may be what kept them away from their abuser for a time. They may start to lose interest in these activities and become isolated from the world around them.

- Questioning their reality - Trauma bonds are often so intense that victims begin to question their reality. The abuser will often make excuses for their behavior, such as blaming the victim for their abusive behavior or making subtle threats that outsiders do not usually note.

- Become more neglectful - Victims in trauma bonds often neglect themselves and their needs, causing them to become less self-aware.

- Become more anxious - When a person is abused and trapped, anxiety becomes a problem. They may feel paranoid or scared of what could happen if they leave. They may also develop debilitating anxiety attacks that prevent them from living normal lives.

- Forget about who they are and what they represent - It is common for victims in trauma bonds to lose their identity. They may lose track of who they are and what they believe in, which will lead to them becoming confused about themselves.

- Becoming controlling - Many people who have experienced trauma bonds find themselves trapped in the cycle of controlling and abusing others out of fear. Often this can occur when an individual's self-esteem is low or when their partner holds onto some form of power over them. For example, if a experiences abuse at the school they attend, they may feel that it is only right that they are allowed to control other people in their lives. This can be a way of controlling themselves and others through fear.

CHAPTER 7: SUBTLE SYMPTOMS OF TRAUMA BONDING

T rauma bonds are often very hard to identify and understand. This is because they occur gradually and yet become so intense that the individual feels powerless to intervene in what is happening. Many individuals might not identify that they are trapped in one of these bonds.

When a person is trapped in a trauma bond, they may exhibit a variety of symptoms, many of which are not immediately apparent. However, the earlier a trauma bond can be identified, the faster an individual can begin working on their recovery and getting out of the situation once and for all.

The following are some of the most prevalent indications that someone is stuck in a trauma bond. It's critical to be aware of these warning signs:

They receive constant criticism

Constant criticism is often the first sign that someone may be in a trauma bond. This criticism can lead to very few moments of affection or no affection at all. The constant criticism can also take the form of a lack of respect from their partner, leading to humiliation. This can happen either in front of people or behind closed doors. The abuser will use constant criticism to tear down the self-esteem of their partner. Constant criticism can be very hurtful and is one of the most prominent signs that an individual has been abused or is being abused.

Constant and harsh criticisms of every decision they make

Similarly, if an individual is presented with a problem and is criticized for their solution, they might begin to feel trapped in their relationship and feel as if they have no control in their life. Constant and harsh criticisms of every decision give an individual the feeling that they have no say in anything.

Unpredictable moods and sudden decisions made by an abusive partner

Unpredictable moods and sudden decisions by an abusive partner will drastically impact a relationship. This may include hot/cold emotions, physical illness after fights, and staying away from home for days at a time. Unpredictable moods and sudden decisions often signify that the abuser is also experiencing traumatic moments.

Irrational outbursts of rage

Irrational outbursts of rage are also signs that someone has been abused or is being abused. These are sudden, emotional, and physical outbursts of rage that can sometimes be directed towards family members or other individuals. These outbursts' emotional and physical nature can lead to serious consequences for an individual who is trapped in a trauma bond.

Acting out in other destructive ways

When individuals have a trauma bond, they might begin acting out in other destructive ways such as abusing drugs or alcohol, gambling, developing eating disorders, and more. This can be a way to cope with the emotional pain they are feeling.

Withdrawal from outside friends and family

Withdrawal from outside friends and family is also a sign that an individual has experienced abuse or is being abused. When an individual feels trapped, they often withdraw from their support network. This can exacerbate their feelings of isolation, as they are no longer receiving the necessary support. An individual who has a trauma bond will often rely on their partner for support, which can lead to further abuse.

If you recognize yourself in any of the above, it is important to do whatever it takes to get out of the abusive situation. It is often the little things that people can do that help to fight the abuse in their relationships. For example, if an individual feels like a partner is not respecting their boundaries, they should call them out on this. They should also not accept any apologies from their partner and instead speak about what happened in order to try and understand.

The Role of the Victim

There are many misconceptions about why victims stay in abusive relationships, and there are also many misconceptions about who stays in abusive relationships. People often will claim that an abused person stayed because they liked the abuse. Other people believe that the abused person stayed because they were weak, or dependent on the abuser.

However, it is much more complicated than this. Victims of abuse stay in their relationships for several reasons – many of which have nothing to do with strength. These reasons include:

- They love their partner, and their partner loves them;

the victim believes that the violence is temporary and will go away.

- Because they are financially reliant on their partner, the victim feels trapped in the relationship. Many of these victims would have no job, money, or any way to support themselves if they left.

- The victim fears retaliation from their abuser if they leave. They fear their abuser may try to hurt them further or even kill them or someone else close to them. This idea comes from the fact that many abusers use threats to keep their partners close to them – threatening harm to a family member or other loved one or even threatening to commit suicide if the victim leaves.

- Many abused people have been taught that they are worthless, and their abuser is the only person who could ever love them. Because of this belief, they can't fathom leaving and being on their own.

- A victim thinks that the abuse is their fault. They believe that if they were more of a certain thing (sexually, emotionally, etc.), the abuse would stop. Many victims believe that if they leave, their partner will find someone else who meets all of their criteria for a spouse/partner.

- Many victims believe that staying and working with their partner is the best way to deal with the abuse.

It is also important to remember how common domestic violence is. One in four women and one in seven men in the United States experience domestic violence before their 18th birthday. According to the National Institute of Justice, 57% of all female murder victims are killed by a current or former husband or boyfriend.

It is often the goal of the abuser to make it so the victim is afraid to leave because they have no way of supporting themselves or their children. In this type of case, leaving will not result in death or being killed, but it may be dangerous for the victim and their children nonetheless – which means that leaving will be a very difficult decision to make.

Stop blaming victims for remaining in abusive relationships is the most effective way to help them. Victims are sometimes left feeling guilty about not leaving, and sometimes they don't truly want to leave; however, it is important for this not to be interpreted as a weak choice by those around them.

What to Watch for When in a Relationship

It is important to pay attention to warning signs that your relationship may be abusive. If you believe you are in an abusive relationship, you should reach out for help and talk about it.

Many organizations can help people being abused and help them take steps to move forward with their lives – even if they do not want to leave the situation.

It is important to know the following signs to determine if you or someone you know if in an abusive relationship. Some of these signs are physical abuse – which means that one person intentionally hurts another person physically:

- Isolation from friends or family members

- Controlling behaviors from the abuser, including jealous tendencies and constantly checking up on their partner

- The abuser using threats to scare their partner into doing what they want

- Physically hurting their partner or threatening to do so in a serious way (e.g., smashing things or stabbing objects near their partner)

- A lack of expression on the face of the abuser. This is a very serious sign of abuse; it shows that the abuser has become emotionally disconnected from the victim.

- Apologizing for hurting their partner and making excuses for doing so after they have done it.

- Making up excuses or not apologizing and getting away with it

- Acting as though they are above authority or looking down on others (this is a sign of someone who feels entitled to do whatever they please and has no regard for other people)

- Blaming their partner for everything that goes wrong in their life and doing nothing to fix it themselves

- Becoming angry at their partner for no reason or showing no empathy for their pain

- Being selfish and not respecting the needs of others

- Telling lies, sometimes continuously, to avoid responsibility. They may also keep secrets from others to keep themselves out of trouble. This is a sign of someone who doesn't trust the people around them. This can be extremely dangerous as many victims do not realize that what they are experiencing is abuse until it's too late.

- Initiating arguments with their partner to get out of doing something or because they want attention, even if this means being mean or yelling at their partner. This is very common in abusive relationships but can be hard to spot unless one pays attention. People who go through this should reach out for help right away.

- Treating their partner as if they were worthless and not caring about them

The previous signs are behaviors that someone in an abusive relationship may see from their partner. Some are much harder to detect, but if a person is paying attention, one or both of their partner's attempts to mentally and emotionally control them can be detected.

The Detachment and Feeling of Invincibility Syndrome

The detachment and feeling of invincibility syndrome (DFICS) of abusive individuals can be one of the most dangerous traits, especially if they have children with their partner. Unfortunately, abuse is a learned behavior, and most abusers were abused themselves. The need to control others happens when an abuser feels worthless. To make up for these feelings, they will manipulate their partners in any way they can to prove that they are powerful.

Abusers are extremely selfish. They only care about themselves. This makes them do whatever it takes to get what they want – including hurting others or being selfish in other ways (e.g., taking all the money in a relationship). The abuser only cares about feeling good and getting what they want in the end.

Many abusers have no remorse for the things that they do. They are often very good at putting on masks to make themselves seem like normal people who care about others. However, behind closed doors, this is not the case at all. They may act differently in public or toward family members but do things to isolate their partner in private where nobody can see what's going on.

People who are abused may fear and love their abuser simultaneously, which can make the abuse even worse. They think they cannot live without them and will do anything to make them happy and keep them around. This sense of feeling trapped is very dangerous, especially if the abuser is emotionally and physically abusive towards their partner, as it will only get worse as time goes on.

The abuser's need to control often leads to arguments because they want to be in charge of everything from what a partner wears to where they go to who their friends are. The abuser may have very strict rules for their partner to follow, making it very difficult for them to move past the abuse. They believe that the abuser will only put up with so much before they walk out and leave them behind.

The abuser will never listen to their partner when they talk about a problem that bothers them. Instead, they will make excuses or blame them for what goes wrong in their relationship. They may also tell many lies and excuses to avoid taking responsibility for their mistakes. This is a clear sign of an abuser and can be very obvious if someone is paying attention.

Abusers will often get angry over nothing or feel like their partner has done something wrong, even if the victim of abuse hasn't done the act they are accused of doing. They will blame their partner for many things, including things out of their control. An abuser will never show any empathy towards their partner (or anyone else) and will make excuses for their abusive behavior, never accepting that anything wrong with their behavior, and never apologizing.

If someone has been abused, there can be many different reasons why it happened. Many abusers have deep-rooted psychological problems and are truly unaware of how abusive their behavior is towards others because of how far down the rabbit hole they have gone.

CHAPTER 8: WHAT STRENGTHENS AND WHAT WEAKENS A TRAUMA BOND

Over time, the trauma Bonding will become stronger, taking a toll on the victim. This is because the bonding process is perpetuated by traumatic events. The victim's ability to see their partner objectively becomes more difficult as the relationship progresses. If a trauma bond is created, it is difficult, if not impossible, for the victim to break free. Trauma bonds enable one person to completely dominate another and have full control over every aspect of their life.

Negative and Inadequate Self-care

The victim's sense of obligation to care for their partner is one of the most common characteristics of the trauma bond. This is often referred to as "enabling." When a victim feels guilty because they cannot assist their partner or are making excuses for their partner's behavior, this can prevent them from taking care of themselves. For example, if an abuser spends too much time at the office or has problems with drug abuse and alcoholism, their partner may make excuses for them or attempt to help them. They may also make decisions that accommodate the abuser's needs and prevent them from leaving.

Another aspect of enabling is that a victim thinks that if they do not take care of their partner, the partner will abandon them. This is a common misconception and often contributes to the continuation of abuse. If the victim wants to end their relationship, they can use a number of strategies to help them in this process. These include:

- Ending unbalanced power games in their relationship by not allowing one person to dictate every aspect of their life. Victims should learn to advocate for themselves and set boundaries on what they need and want.

- Detaching from their relationship. They can no longer allow their partner to be the source of their happiness. This is easier said than done, but if partners feel like they are dependent on their relationship for stability, they will often remain in a toxic relationship.

-

Praying or meditating to find comfort and strength.

- Joining a support group to help them further detach from the bond and deal with any trauma they have experienced.

- Communicating with friends and family members to see what resources and support systems are available to them. These people will often listen without judgment and support victims in whatever decision they make regarding the relationship.

- Seeking out a therapist or other professional who can help them process their thoughts and emotions and give them a healthy perspective on the relationship. Professional help is available to assist victims in understanding the trauma bond and how it affects their lives.

- Not feeling guilty for leaving or breaking up with their partner. Abusers often use guilt and shame to keep victims attached to a toxic relationship. If they are able and safe, they should immediately leave the abuser.

Financial Dependence

Some victims are financially dependent on their partners. If they do not make enough money, they may not be able to pay the rent or meet basic needs. Abusers may threaten to cut off finances or withhold them altogether if the victims leaves the relationship. Finally, abusers often have access to bank accounts and other financial resources and can cause serious damage to victims who leave the relationship. Financial dependence can prevent victims from taking care of themselves in various ways due to threats of financial destruction, lack of employment opportunities, manipulation, and more.

The only way to break the bond is for a victim to break free from their financial dependence. This can be done by:

- Leaving the relationship if a partner will not work and contribute financially.

- Not allowing their partner to control the financial aspects of their life such as bank accounts, credit cards, loans, and more.

- Developing a budget to see where they are spending their money and making financial decisions independently.

- Receiving or taking out loans or credit cards to provide for themselves

- Having an emergency fund to deal with financial emergencies when necessary.

- Accepting donations from friends and family. Seeking

financial assistance from other sources is an important step towards recovery from the trauma bond and can help victims meet their needs.

- Acting as a friend or advocate for themselves. Often, people allow their finances to be controlled by others because they do not have anyone they trust enough to advocate on their behalf.

- Victims should not feel guilty for leaving or breaking up with their partner if they are refusing to contribute financially. Abusers often use guilt and shame to keep victims attached to a toxic relationship.

Social/Cultural Values

Family values and cultural norms play a prominent role in our society. Many people believe that couples should put the stability of their relationship beyond their own happiness. They believe that if a spouse is abusive, they should stay with them and work through their problems. These are often the same people who say that marriage is sacred and vow to "love, honor, cherish" until death. They often feel that there is something fundamentally wrong with the victim for leaving their partner.

These same people may also believe that it will create a "broken home" if the victim leaves the abusive relationship. They may believe that children should always be with their biological parents. It is true that if a child is raised in a broken home, it can have an adverse effect on their development. However, this does not necessarily mean that children always benefit from being raised in a two-parent home. If there are problems in the home, it can also negatively impact their development.

This way of thinking can also be expressed by the family and friends of the victim. As a result, the victim may feel like they have no one in their corner. If a friend or family member tries to make them see their point of view, it usually makes them feel worse about themselves and their situation. Many victims feel that they are always walking on eggshells so that no one is upset with them. They believe that if they say something or do something wrong, they will be blamed for the problems in the relationship. This can be very difficult to deal with emotionally and psychologically.

The truth is that many people do not understand the dynamics of a domestic violence relationship. They think that couples should work through their problems and practice togetherness. They do not realize that abuse in a relationship is one-sided, and the abuser often uses their insecurities and issues within themselves as an excuse for their behavior.

This way of thinking is learned from others who think similarly or have similar values. They are also learned from social norms, cultural norms, religious beliefs, etc. When victims of domestic violence hear these opinions from their friends, family members, and others, they internalize these messages. They begin to think that this is what it means to be a community member.

When we have these perceptions of right or wrong within our culture and society, we often judge others for not behaving in certain ways. We may continue this mindset for many years until we connect with someone that makes us begin to question our beliefs. Then, we begin to change how we view others within our culture, society, family, and ourselves. We realize that there are other ways to behave besides those perceived as acceptable by society or those taught in school or through the media. This is when victims of domestic violence realize that they have options and can choose to leave their abusive relationships if they so wish.

Culture, society, family, and friends play an important role in how domestic violence is viewed. It is important to recognize these perceptions and learn how they influence victims of domestic violence.

When victims see domestic abusers getting away with their actions because "it's what you do," it teaches them to view themselves as losers in society. They believe that if they leave their partner, society will turn its back on them because of what has happened to them. The victim believes that if they do not do what their abuser wants, they will be harassed and discriminated against. Many domestic violence victims believe that these things and experiences are part of the "normal" world or life for abuse victims. They believe that they can't obtain a restraining order or divorce. They feel like they can't get away from the abuser because the authorities will not help them, society will not help them, and nobody loves them.

This way of thinking can make victims feel extremely hopeless. They may believe they have only a few options and will take whatever they can get.

This way of thinking may also help victims justify why the abuse is happening. They believe that when their partners say things like "I'm sorry," "I'll never do it again," and "I just lost my temper," the violence is over. They believe that if they respond in a certain way or act differently in future, the abuse will stop.

This affects how victims live their lives every day. They may become depressed, anxious, and frightened for themselves and others, as well as for their families.

It is important to learn the dynamics of domestic violence in relationships and how these relationships are viewed by society, family, friends, and the victims themselves.

Emotional Dependence

Victims can become emotionally dependent on their abuser to an extent that they cannot express their emotions without feeling guilty or ashamed. They may feel wrong or bad for feeling angry, depressed, or sad. If they express these emotions, the abuser will often make them feel guilty and responsible for any negative feelings, leaving victims feeling helpless and incapable of expressing themselves. Emotional dependence is a common phenomenon within relationships. However, it is currently not fully understood and not discussed in-depth, even among professional psychologists.

Victims will often fear their abuser becoming angry if they express these feelings, but no one should be afraid to express their emotions. There may be times when victims are not certain about which feelings to express, but they should speak up in this situation nonetheless. Victims of abuse need to learn to express themselves and their emotions even when it may be hard.

However, when victims have been abused for a long time, it can be difficult for them to fully understand their own emotions. It is even more difficult for them to understand what others' emotions are trying to tell them. If a victim constantly feels angry or depressed but doesn't know why, that is a sign of emotional dependence on an abuser. Victims need to learn that people can experience these emotions for various reasons, and they don't necessarily mean that anything is wrong with them.

Victims of domestic violence can experience negative emotions for various reasons, such as feeling angry at their abuser, feeling ashamed about the abuse or past events surrounding the abuse, love for their abuser, or even fear of their abuser. They may feel these emotions when they are at home together, or they may feel these emotions when spending time with friends and family members.

Victims of domestic violence often feel shame or guilt for expressing these negative emotions. But no one should be held responsible for how they feel while they are getting through the abuse cycle.

Incompatible World Views

After being abused, victims often develop a "don't ask, don't tell" attitude. They may try to pretend that everything is okay and not report the abuse to anyone. They will try to protect the abuser from getting into legal trouble and from the consequences of their actions, sometimes without thinking about what will happen to themselves as result.

This phenomenon is called having an "incompatible world view." Victims who develop this attitude after being abused feel that if they do not hide what their abuser does, the abuser will become angry and violent against them.

Similarly, when victims feel emotionally dependent on their abusers, they may be so afraid of telling others about the abuse that they begin keeping secrets from family members and friends. They will lie and tell others that everything is okay when it isn't.

They may also be ashamed of the relationship or ashamed and embarrassed about the situation at home. Many victims try to keep these secrets for themselves for a long time, and family members and friends may not realize that physical abuse has occurred until the bruises and marks begin to show. As a result, these friends or families will often be critical of them for not reporting the abuse earlier.

Victims often feel insecure about speaking with others about these issues because they want to avoid drama, arguments, fights, or other negative consequences from their abuser.

In conclusion, there are many reasons why abuse victims do not tell anyone about what is happening in their lives. The more victims rest in these unhealthy feelings and beliefs about the world around them, the more emotionally dependent they become on their abusers. This makes it difficult for them to see a way out and move forward with their lives.

The most important thing that victims can do to start moving forward is realizing that they are not alone in this journey.

CHAPTER 9: 9 ESSENTIAL STEPS TO BEGIN BREAKING TRAUMATIC BONDING

Breaking the cycle and getting away from this type of relationship and the abuser who created it can be difficult. However, recognizing the signs that this is happening is the most effective thing you can do. Once you have recognized this, you can take action to get out of it – no matter how hard it is.

People who have been abused often feel like they have been "trapped" in their relationships because of the debilitating effects of their abusers' actions. However, even though this sense of being trapped is very real and understandable, it is wrong to assume that there's some magical trap you can't possibly escape from. The truth is that the only thing standing between you and a healthier relationship is yourself – your strength, integrity, stamina, and ability to take action when necessary.

The Difference Between a Healthy Relationship and a Relationship with an Abuser

Healthy relationships are built on mutual trust, respect, and love. There is a feeling of connectedness to the relationship, and there is nothing forced or fake about it. The relationship as a whole is healthy and positive, and both parties are in agreement about what is going on between them.

This isn't to say that there won't be difficulties or disagreements; however, these issues can be discussed without anger or resentment on either side. Both people can agree with the decisions made once an issue arises without any trouble, even if these decisions benefit one partner over the other.

This type of relationship is built on a stable foundation and grows over time, which means that it is not built exclusively on "good times" or a series of amazing events. Instead, it is built on each partner's everyday actions and behaviors within the relationship itself. If both partners are happy and satisfied with their connection, neither will feel "trapped" by their connection.

In contrast, a trauma bond occurs when two people are connected by mental/emotional abuse. They are connected due to trauma – but not in a healthy way at all.

Trauma bonds are built through terrorism, hurt, and pain. They are based on feelings of confusion, despair, and hopelessness within both partners – which means that there is no light at the end of the tunnel for either person in this type of relationship. Both partners suffer alone, despite being together. This "together" aspect is very important when it involves an abuser because both partners believe they can depend on each other to go through all negative experiences together, including abuse and neglect. It can be very hard to end this relationship, even when both partners know it isn't healthy.

The difference between a trauma bond (relationship built on mental/emotional abuse) and a healthy adult relationship comes down to trust, respect, love, and connection. Without trust, respect, love, and connection as a foundation of a relationship, the relationship will not be healthy. It will probably end in either divorce or abuse (and sometimes both), which shows how important it is to have a healthy foundation.

If you leave an abusive relationship, you may believe that you will never be able to trust another person again. Yes, it can take time to rebuild trust and feel safe with another partner – but it is a process that anyone can achieve.

Breaking the Cycle of Trauma Bonding

To break the cycle of trauma bonding, you must work towards finding your strength and becoming able to confront the abuser. Remind yourself that it is not your fault that you feel afraid, confused, or unhappy. Building up your trust in yourself will help you ultimately get through abuse without being controlled by it. If someone is abusing you, you can work towards building a sense of self and breaking the cycle by following these steps:

1. Identify when abuse occurs and how it is being done.

When being attacked, listen to what the person is saying and pay attention to their tone. Their voice may be sarcastic and mean-spirited if they try to hurt you. They may be using negative words meant to put you down or to make them look like they are somehow better than you. If this is happening, it means that their real intent is not to love or help you but only to control and hurt you.

2. Demand respect from the other person by telling them that you need some time alone.

Suppose they ask why. Tell them that you need time to collect your thoughts and feelings. Start thinking about how you feel and what you want for yourself. You may want to write down all of the things the abuser has done or said so that you can see it clearly, instead of letting it muddle up your mind.

3. Work towards building your self-confidence so that you are not looking to your abuser for your sense of self-worth.

This is your number one priority because it is the key to dealing with trauma bonding, whether it involves emotional or physical abuse. You must love yourself before another person can begin to love you. This can take time and support from friends/family, but it is possible to achieve if you put your mind to it.

4. Do not let them make excuses for their actions towards you.

Suppose they tell you that they were angry when a specific incident happened – do not believe this because it's a lie designed to hurt you more deeply. Ask yourself if there were other ways that this situation could have been handled.

5. Work on getting over your emotional abuse issues so that you can leave the relationship.

You must work towards accepting yourself and having realistic self-confidence. You will then be able to leave and regain some independence.

6. Accept that leaving a person can be painful, but it is worth all the pain.

When telling the other person that you are leaving them, it may be difficult to keep from crying – but you must convey your feelings. If they make any excuse for what they've done (or for not doing something) let them know that you do not believe anything they are saying and leave the room or house immediately before retaliating.

This is a good opportunity to find someone who will support you and help you through this extremely difficult time in your life. This may be a family member or close friend, but it's also possible to make new friends or start a support group for other people trying to leave emotional abuse behind.

7. Maintain your self-respect and dignity.

When leaving an emotional abuser, feel proud of yourself and do not think that you failed in any way by doing this. Even if it's difficult to admit that the other person was hurting you (or manipulating you) and that at times you put your needs last to make them feel better about themselves, you did the right thing by finally standing up for yourself. You may have to face some pretty distressing feelings when leaving an emotional abuser, but the benefit of beating this is greater than any amount of pain or regret you might experience.

8. Do not try and change your partner

Accept that your partner is not going to change, and they are not going to suddenly love you, but they can learn to respect you and treat you better than they did before. Focus instead on what you can do for yourself, and learn to put yourself first.

9. Don't stay silent.

If you are being abused, talk to someone about it. This may be a teacher, friend, or parent, your pastor; or a social worker, counselor, or psychologist – the list goes on and varies depending on where the abuse is occurring in your life.

The best thing for both parties to do is get some help before things get worse. This may mean that you need to be assertive and tell them how their behavior affects you, but if they are not amenable to change, you must think about what is best for you and get out of this situation as soon as possible.

The effects of being emotionally abused can last a long time after the relationship has ended. It's important to avoid becoming isolated by staying in touch with your friends, family, and other people who care about you.

Seek Professional Help

It is important to seek professional help if the emotional abuse continues or the effects of the trauma become severe, such as suicidal thoughts, death threats, or an assault.

You may want to contact a counselor or therapist. Counselors can assist you in putting aside your feelings about the abuse and helping you to think about what is best for your own goals and personal growth. Someone trained to deal with abusive situations can help you determine how long it might take for you to get better, what kind of relationship you might be able to have with your partner if they stop abusing you, and whether divorce is a good idea or not.

A counselor or therapist may also help you learn how to manage your emotions after being abused. Finally, a counselor can help you decide if you want to return to the relationship once it seems safe.

As we know, many people who have been emotionally abused will become isolated. This can lead to depression, self-contempt, and other issues that make it difficult for victims to function. Speaking with someone about your feelings can help you deal with them.

Some people do not want to seek professional help because they do not want to face emotions that they may be repressing. Others, however, avoid seeking professional help because they cannot afford it. If you cannot afford to go to therapy, you may consider joining a support group. This can help you talk out you problems with other people who have been in the same situation and understand how you feel.

These days, many online services offer counseling. Although this may not be as helpful as face-to-face counseling or therapy, it is still possible for them to offer some benefit. Many of these services offer phone or chat support for victims of abuse that live in another state or country.

Emotional abuse can have lasting effects on an individual, a couple, or a family. Because of this, anyone who has been emotionally abused should seek professional help.

PART 3
- LIBERATING YOURSELF FROM A TRAUMATIC BOND

CHAPTER 10: ADMITTING THAT YOU HAVE A TRAUMA BOND

Before you can begin to break the trauma bond, you must first be aware of its presence. You may find it difficult to admit that you have a trauma bond with your partner or ex-partner. And even though you logically may know that the relationship is/was unhealthy and destructive, your feelings may contradict your conscious thoughts and feelings. Or perhaps you are so emotionally fused with your partner that your learned helplessness keeps you feeling powerless to change things.

When you first realize that you are in a trauma bond

You start to feel angry, anxious, or afraid. You might be overwhelmed with sadness and despair. Or you might feel like running away physically or mentally. The intense pain can leave you feeling numb and disconnected from yourself. You may even begin to wonder if life is worth living.

You may think that you have caused your partner's abuse, but this is far from the truth. Your new awareness of your trauma bond will start to bring forth the truth that you have been living in a dysfunctional relationship. The trauma bond's signs, symptoms, and behaviors will communicate that the relationship is unhealthy and abusive.

You might be angry at your partner for hurting you. You might feel like terminating the relationship. You may even have urges to kill your partner or express hatred towards them. These are all natural reactions when entering this stage of awareness. After all, you are not in control of your mind or heart at this point. You have been stripped of any power or authority over your life and body and have been reduced to a powerless and subservient state.

Your feelings will tell you that your relationship is destructive and unhealthy, but your heart is speaking. You have spent all of your life in denial (learned helplessness), and now it has taken over. You cannot change what has happened, and you can only learn from this painful experience while allowing yourself to be healed by the pain of the trauma bond and healing process.

Becoming Aware of Your Triggers and Patterns

It will help if you become aware of how you react in your relationship with your partner and how you may have co-created this abusive dynamic. It is important to learn how you perpetuate the trauma bond and abuse cycle, what parts of the drama are familiar to you, how you contribute to the drama, and how much control you maintain over your reactions. This can be painful because you it forces you to see the truth about how your partner caused you to act. You may have been in denial of this truth for much of your life.

But it is time to stop the lies and deception once and for all. You have a human right to be treated with respect, dignity, appreciation, love, and kindness.

Ask yourself why you have stayed with your partner or ex-partner. Before you can end your trauma bond, you must first know what is happening and how this trauma bond has been formed.

Because you were taught to only see things in black and white, it may be difficult for you to see the good in anyone. Even though you may not feel anything good about your partner or ex-partner right now, recognize that there are positive traits in them.

List all the positive things about your partner or ex-partner

1

____

2

____

3

____

4

____

5

____

It is also possible that you have been brainwashed into believing that your abusive partner is perfect and thus worthy of being loved unconditionally by you. If this is the case, do not dismiss or deny that their bad behavior reflects their negative traits or characteristics.

List the reasons or reasons why you do not see the good in your partner/ex-partner

1

____

2

____

3

____

4

____

5

____

Compare this list to the positive traits you listed above and decide if they are more important to you than their negative traits or characteristics. The reason for this exercise is that you must decide whether your partner or ex-partner's positive traits are better than their negative traits. This will help you decide whether your relationship is worth saving or if it's time to call it quits.

The goal here is to do what is best for yourself, which means examining and analyzing the situation with a clear mind. If you are unwilling to look at both their good and bad traits honestly and without bias, it would be best to end the relationship now instead of later when emotions run high, and you are stuck in the drama.

If your partner's or ex-partner's good traits outweigh their bad traits, then you may decide to stay with them. You can do this by ignoring the bad behavior and only rewarding the good behavior if you are one of those people who believes in positive reinforcement.

Although this does work for some people, others may find that ignoring the bad behavior does not work. Do not feel that you have failed as a partner if ignoring the bad behavior does not work for you. Instead, try other approaches such as talking to your partner while calm, encouraging healthy behaviors, discouraging unwanted behaviors, etc.

Emotions and Trauma Bonding

You may be unable to see your partner's or ex-partner's bad traits because of your low self-esteem issues, codependency issues, etc. If this is the case, these issues need to be addressed first. It may be easier for you to see your partner's manipulation for what it is by addressing your mental health first. You may also find that their manipulation no longer works on you because you are now more aware of it.

Fortunately for those manipulated through a trauma bond, they can break free from the manipulation if they truly want to do so. The abuser or their negative behaviors may no longer threaten you because you are aware of the manipulation now.

You must want to truly break free from a trauma bond in order to do so. If you stay in a relationship because of your partner's or ex-partner's negative behavior, then you may feel emotionally manipulated and controlled. You may need to leave that relationship for your sanity. You may also find yourself trapped in an apparently never-ending cycle of leaving and returning to the same relationship. This can ruin your life and can make you feel like there is "no way out" of this situation.

If both you and your partner or ex-partner have codependency issues, low self-esteem issues, etc., there is still hope that this trauma bond can be broken, however, it will take time and patience. You will also need the support of professionals who can help you deal with your codependency issues, low self-esteem issues, etc.

You are solely responsible for your own life and choices. You can choose to stay or go. You can choose not to be held hostage in your relationship by a trauma bond. You can be strong enough to walk away from your partner or ex-partner if that is what you want. It may take time to heal, but it is possible.

Beginning a New Relationship

Although the abusive relationship may be over on paper and at home, you may still dream about your ex-partner. Sometimes, however, you will meet someone new to whom you start to feel attracted. In this case, it is prudent to discuss these dreams with someone prior to entering another relationship. Also discuss your reasons for being attracted to this other person before getting involved physically. Doing so may save you from heartbreak in the future.

After talking to someone, you can decide whether or not you want to be involved with this other person. If you choose to get involved with them, it is time to stop focusing on the past and truly focus on your needs and wants. However, it is important to watch carefully to ensure you have not inadvertently entered another abusive relationship. Your new partner might suddenly change their behavior or start acting differently towards you. This could show up in many ways, as though they have a trauma bond with someone else. Suddenly, they start acting in ways that they never acted before. The two of you split up and get back together over and over again.

This can feel like a roller coaster ride with an endpoint that you cannot find. After you have been through this for a while, you may notice that your self-esteem issues are returning. You may feel like your life is a mess due to this relationship. Your new trauma bond will keep you stuck in this relationship and prevent you from truly moving on and finding happiness in your life.

If you are in this situation, you should consult a professional who can help you solve your issues.

Your partner or ex-partner may have become a negative role model for you, especially if they are repeating their history with someone else. They keep getting involved with people who treat them badly, too, and moving from one failed relationship to another over and over again.

This is a highly complicated subject that involves numerous variables and can be extremely traumatic for anyone involved in this type of relationship. If you have codependency issues and low self-esteem issues, it would be best to talk to someone about them to help you get better.

CHAPTER 11: SEEKS SUPPORT TO CREATE A SAFE EXIT

A side from working on our recovery, it is also important for victims to plan a way out of the relationship. Once again, this means taking action based on an informed decision. This may also entail changing your social circle. We all have many people in our lives who may know our situation, which can make recovery difficult at times. It is normal to feel isolated and nauseous when you contact these people, but don't feel like you need to explain everything in order for them to be supportive. Their support of you is already there, and they will not abandon you. Your job is to tell them what has happened and let them know how safe you are now.

The First Step Toward Severing a Trauma Bond

The first step toward leaving a toxic relationship is usually to seek out support from an outside person. Unfortunately, friends and family often do not know you are involved in a trauma bond and are likely to react skeptically or doubtfully. This is because the experience of a trauma bond is so foreign to the average person that most people don't understand it, even many therapists. Therefore, seeking support from friends and family can be frustrating and disheartening. It is important to remember that you are the expert on your trauma, and those who do not understand it may react with only their own experiences in mind.

It is vital to seek support from someone outside the relationship and understand the dynamics of a trauma bond. If you can find at least one person to support you, even if they don't fully understand what has happened, you are on your way to recovery, and your exit will be a lot easier.

Sharing With Others

It is important to remember that everyone operates with their own experiences and assumptions. Just because someone doesn't understand your situation doesn't mean they don't care. It can be helpful to keep the following things in mind when seeking support from others:

- The reactions of friends and family to the news of your abuse can be unpredictable, and you may feel hurt or confused. But their reactions do not have to determine how you feel about yourself, and being understood is often more important than being validated by them.

- The people who love you will show their love by taking the time to understand and give you the needed support.

- You need to take care of yourself during this time. Make sure your needs are being met, and make sure others respect your boundaries.

- You may already have a network in place with people in your life who will be supportive and understanding; recognize it and use it when you need to.

- Know that there is no need to explain or justify your actions. Recovery is not based on the rules of society, so do whatever you need to do to make yourself feel safe and happy.

- Respect that others may not understand the dynamics of a trauma bond; they might try to assure you that what you are experiencing is normal. Remember that they are learning more about something they don't understand, so they may need to ask many questions, and it may feel like they are probing. Let them ask the questions and try not to take them personally.

- Remember that even if you are the only one in your life who knows what happened, others will likely find out and begin to think they know more than they do. At that point, it is okay to let them know what has happened to you if you feel you will benefit from sharing.

- You may need to explain just how safe you are, why you are safe, and how you know you are safe. Additionally, you may need to reassure them that this is not the case in the past.

- If people react with disbelief, just move on. If they don't want to believe it, that's not your problem. Remember that the actions of others do not have any bearing on your sense of self and what has happened in a situation.

It is important to remember that the reactions of others are often a reflection of the way they think and feel. Don't hold their reactions against them, and don't let them hurt your feelings by thinking they don't support you. Take care of yourself and seek out a secure location to heal from trauma bonding.

The Triggers and How to Overcome Them

Trauma bonding has a lot of triggers. Some of these include:

- Having a fantasy that the relationship will change and suddenly become healthy, stable, and nurturing. It is important to realize that this will never happen. Your fantasies about what the relationship could be are not going to happen. This keeps you involved with an abusive person or in an abusive situation.

- Being triggered by betrayal or fear that your partner will leave the relationship if you don't comply with everything they want from you or do for them. It is extremely important to remember that abuse is not a sign of true love. A healthy partner will not and cannot control or own you, and they will never put you in a position to destroy yourself.

- Being led to believe that you are the only one who can help your abuser overcome the problems they are experiencing. You are not responsible for their health or happiness – your abuser is responsible for themselves. If you want to help someone else heal, be sure it isn't at your own expense.

- Fearing that eating disorders, mental illness, suicide attempts, or other destructive behavior will happen if you leave the relationship. You are not accountable for your abuser's actions or struggles, and they are not accountable for you.

- Having a belief that abuse or trauma bonding is normal. It is not. The abuse is abnormal, and the trauma bond can be as well. Acknowledge that your situation it was never "natural" nor "normal," and that you are free to leave the relationship.

- Having a fear that you will become sick or crazy if you leave the relationship. This is not true. It is never your responsibility to fix someone else's problems, nor should it ever be considered as a legitimate reason to stay with an abusive person.

- Feeling guilty because you feel like you're betraying your partner, their family, or their culture if you end the relationship.

- Feeling responsible for your abuser's well-being. You are not responsible for their well-being. And it does not matter what constitutes a "personal problem" for them because you don't need to be there to determine that.

- Fearing the pain of making an important decision on your own.

Making the Decision to Leave

Regularly check in with yourself about whether you're staying in an abusive or unhealthy relationship, and whether it's time to leave. You can ask yourself the following questions:

Do I feel stuck?

Do you feel as though you are forced to stay in a relationship against your will, or because you want it to change or need it for health reasons like having someone who cares for you or your children?

Do I feel that something must change within the relationship?

If so, the first thing is to gather more information so you can make a better decision at the end of the day.

Am I getting any benefit from being in this relationship?

Regardless of what your partner may have led you to believe, you cannot get anything out of a relationship if someone uses you and abuses you simultaneously.

Do I feel as if my life is in danger?

Do you feel as though your life is threatened by someone trying to make you do something you do not want to do? This means that they will never allow you to live your life the way you want and can force you into doing things you don't wish to do.

Do I feel accepted?

Why would one stay in a relationship where they're not accepted? To be happy in a relationship, your partner must accept you for who you truly are.

Do I feel as if I am being neglected?

You deserve to be someone's priority. You deserve love and care. It's important to have a good foundation in life where honesty and respect are key factors within a relationship.

Am I willing to compromise?

You can compromise with your emotions and effectively express yourself with all of the changes in a relationship every day. Still, some people do not want to do this because they are angry or emotional.

Sometimes you have to let go of someone who doesn't deserve your time, energy, or love. You have to accept the fact that it's not your fault that you were abused, and it's never your responsibility to make up for someone else's abusive behavior.

You can regain control by getting out of the relationship and getting help from trusted friends and family members.

Listening to Your Inner Voice and Making a Plan

The best way to get out of an abusive relationship is to listen to your inner voice and plan. Consider the following steps:

- Firstly, consider all the options you have in a situation.

- Get help from friends and family members who can help you get out of an abusive relationship.

- Talk with someone you trust about whether leaving the relationship is the right thing for you or not.

- Get out of the situation, stay out for a little while, and see what happens. If you change your mind and go back to the relationship, you're classifying yourself as someone who permits abuse.

- Move on with your life. If you decide to do nothing, you will lose further control of yourself and will likely give up before long.

Getting Involved in Activities That Help You Focus on Yourself

If you stay active and involved with the people who care about you, it will be easier for you to leave the abusive relationship. This means taking action by getting help from someone who can protect and support you. You have to remember that getting out of an abusive relationship is a process, so don't try to do everything at once.

The following are activities you can focus on to help yourself leave an abusive relationship:

- Attend physical and emotional therapy to help you heal.

- Get in touch with your friends and family members who can help you heal.

- Go to a support group.

- Take long walks with your pet or a friend.

- Play sports, watch a movie, or even listen to music while you're alone.

- Go shopping, read magazines, or do other things that make you happy to break the negative energy of the situation.

- Write in a journal about your experiences, thoughts, and feelings; this helps you get out of an abusive relationship and start healing from trauma bonding.

- Start eating better, sleeping more, and exercising to help you break out of the abusive cycle and heal yourself from trauma.

- Know that you deserve help from someone who can support you with your interests, needs, and recovery.

It is possible to get out of an abusive relationship and find a supportive person to help you get better and be happy. This can be difficult, but it's well worth the effort. Everything will be okay in time if you take action, give yourself a break, and let go of the past so it won't destroy your future.

Changing the Focus of Your Thoughts and Feelings

When you have trauma bonding, it's hard to focus on other things in life. You have to stop focusing on the abusive relationship and focus on your happiness. When you focus on yourself and let go of the past, it will be easier to heal from the abuse and move on with your life.

You have to remember that you deserve to be happy and have the life you desire. You don't want the abuse to define who you are, so focus on the things that bring you joy and happiness.

If you focus on yourself, it will be easier for you to leave an abusive relationship.

It is possible to focus on the positive things in life without feeling trapped by an abusive relationship and the pain that comes with it.

The happiest people are satisfied with their own lives, and they tend not to become involved in abusive relationships. They feel lucky that they don't have an abusive partner and do everything they can to make their lives better and free from abuse of any kind.

CHAPTER 12: "WHAT'S WRONG WITH ME" OR "THIS IS MY FAULT"- STOP SELF-BLAME

Self-blame is common in trauma victims, particularly those who have endured childhood abuse. It manifests in self-destructive behaviors, including drug and alcohol addiction, eating disorders, and compulsive shopping habits. Self-blaming thoughts like "what's wrong with me" or "this is my fault" create a cycle of mental illness that traps the victim in an endless spiral of low self-esteem. To break this cycle and finally find peace with oneself, it's important to acknowledge the presence of these thoughts (and feelings). You can then recognize that they are not true and finally come to terms with their root cause (abuse) and the present-day ramifications of being abused in the past.

Victims should not feel guilty because they were subjected to abuse. After all, it was not their fault. Guilt, fears and self-hatred often prevent victims from connecting with others and forming healthy relationships. Ultimately, self-blame must be overcome so that the victim can enter a new phase of healing where they can finally find peace with themselves and recover from trauma bonding.

Stop Blaming Yourself for the Abusive Situation

It's easy for victims to blame themselves for the abusive situation, especially if they were abused by someone close to them. But you should not be held accountable for someone else's actions. The blame belongs to your abuser, not you. You must move past self-blame and realize that the abusive situation occurred because of them.

No matter what happened in your past, you are not responsible for your actions. Simply forgiving the person will help you let go of the anger and fear. They do not deserve your forgiveness; but you require it. Once you've forgiven them, you'll find yourself more capable of moving past the abuse and starting a new life free from their influence. You will be able to make healthier choices regarding the relationships you form in the future.

You have no influence over the decisions of others; all you have control over is your own. Choose self-love over self-hate and move on with your life. Do not allow them to continue to oppress you, abuse you, and take away your self-esteem. Acknowledge that the person was once a part of your life but is no longer an active part in it, and accept that you have the freedom to live in peace without them.

People often find it hard to move past trauma because they fear what lies beyond their abusive situation. Despite being mentally or emotionally scarred as a result of their trauma, they want to act as if nothing ever happened. When they think about stepping into a new phase of life without the abuse, they must overcome self-doubt (and often guilt) in order to finally able to overcome the effects of their trauma.

Let Go of Self-Blame by Forgiving Others.

This habit is difficult but liberating. When you forgive others, you move beyond the past. What they did was wrong, but there is no reason why you should hold a grudge against them for the rest of your life. You can't change the past, so why dwell on it? Forgiving someone for an act of abuse is often a tough pill to swallow, but it's necessary to move forward in life and away from your abuser's influence. You can forgive through empathy, giving them the benefit of the doubt that they did not have ill-intentions.

This process requires a certain amount of vulnerability and courage. Forgiving others means acknowledging their suffering and moving on from the trauma bonding. This process is often difficult for people who have been victimized as children but is necessary to ensure your own physical and psychological well-being. It's time to move on with your life and find a brighter future. You were the innocent victim.

The Four Steps of Forgiveness

- Acknowledge the abuse, its consequences, and the fact that it was wrong.

- Admit to yourself that you were wronged by the acts of your abuser and deserve an apology.

- Apologize to yourself for holding on to resentment and anger towards your abuser, even if they do not apologize to you directly or admit their wrongdoing, which often never happens anyway. If they have already apologized to you, thank them for their apology and move on.

- Work on forgiving your abuser. You'll need to be strong and resilient to do this because it doesn't mean you've forgotten what they did or that they now deserve a place in your heart; it means you're no longer letting their actions affect you on a daily basis and that you'll hold them accountable for their actions from now on by refusing to tolerate abuse in any form or living in fear of retaliation for leaving them.

If you choose to confront your abuser, keep in mind that sometimes abusers cannot control their behavior and they may react negatively. If they react badly to your confrontation, then it's best that you cut all ties with them and avoid further confrontation at all costs. Facing someone who has wronged you is intimidating and can bring back memories of being controlled by them that you have worked to overcome.

Once you have left the relationship, it is important to minimize contact with your abuser to protect yourself against further abuse. Suppose your abuser chooses to be a part of your life again by appearing suddenly, emailing you, or calling. In that case, you may need to limit contact with them or prevent them from contacting you in the first place (i.e., unfollowing on social media, removing them from your address book, etc.).

Being in the Right Place, Doing the Right Thing, at the Right Time.

Being in the right place means being in a secure and safe environment where you don't feel as though you are putting yourself at risk. Ensure that you do not engage in risky behaviors such as driving alone at night or having too much to drink around those who abused you in the past.

Doing the right thing means having the courage to confront your abuser and putting an end to their abuse permanently. This may mean having to face them, but you should stop letting them abuse you any longer. It's important to remain calm during the confrontation if possible.

If things escalate, use facts and figures about your abuse instead of reacting with anger or trying to reason with your abuser. If their reaction is not what you expected, turn around and leave immediately. It's important to be assertive and stand up for yourself. Many abusers are very good at preventing other people from caring about their own self-preservation. You must be strong enough not to allow that to happen.

Remember that there is always a way out, even when the odds are stacked against you. If you are not sure what to do, consult with a therapist or counselor who can guide you during this time. They will be able to help provide the support that you need during this difficult time—controlling your reactions and de-escalating the situation when under verbal fire.

- Make sure you have enough time and space to properly deal with this situation.

- Remind yourself that you deserve respect, not being talked down to or having your feelings dismissed by anyone.

- Practice deep breathing techniques, yoga, or any other exercises that can help you calm down before talking to the person who is abusing you. Deep breathing will help with anger and frustration that may arise during a confrontation.

- Ask them why they are saying these things, and make sure they know why their words hurt you so much.

- Tell them that you know they do not mean these things and ask them to stop.

- Remind yourself of the reasons why you are angry and frustrated with the situation, and make sure that you stay focused on the matter at hand so you can make the best decisions.

- Never apologize for your feelings towards their abuse; let them know that you don't have to apologize for your own emotions.

- Say what is necessary and do not justify your actions with excuses such as, "it's a long story."

- Let them know that they have affected you by making you question your self-worth, but they must now realize just how significant this has been in affecting everything else in your life.

- Ask them once again, "Why do you say these things to me?" and make sure they know why this is so important to you.

- Make sure your abuser knows why their abuse is so wrong and hurtful. A strong statement such as "I don't think any comments of yours will ever justify your treatment of me" or "You are leaving me no choice" can be effective in making them feel the consequences of their actions.

- Never show fear or retreat at any time; stand firm in what you believe in, even if it means standing alone.

- Do not back down or give up at any time; keep your composure and respond with facts and figures rather than emotions.

- Be assertive and respectful in handling the situation; do not react with anger or try to reason with your abuser, especially if they try to talk you down.

- Reassure yourself that you will survive this, it's not worth getting abused again, and there is always a way out of an abusive situation – the sooner you get out, the safer everyone involved will be.

Using a Script to Help You Deal with Stress

One of the most difficult parts of trauma recovery is finding ways to deal with stress. You can do lots of different things, like meditation, yoga, or deep breathing exercises, but they don't always work. Sometimes, these things are not enough, and you end up in a worse state than before. You might think that the best way to deal with your stress is to tough it out, grit your teeth and bear it. You may think that being a "tough guy" or "tough gal" will make everything better. But if it doesn't, you get more upset and frustrated. Or you may try to distract yourself. But when the stress becomes too much, even the distraction techniques don't work anymore. There are other things that you can do, though.

One such idea is to write in a journal using a "script." That's a way to tell yourself the story of your trauma over and over again in written form. By repeating an event or the feelings and sensations that go with it, you can learn to relate to those feelings in a new way. Then, when something triggers those feelings again, you have already been through the process several times and can handle it more quickly. This is also called "trauma processing." And if you use it often enough, you may eventually find that those old painful feelings don't come up very often anymore. I've heard people say that the most important part about writing a script is just getting started. It's about getting the words down. The words don't have to be perfect. They help you process your emotions and put them into a pattern that works for you.

A script is a list or outline of what you want to say in response to an emotional trigger and how it will make you feel if it happens again. This is different from just writing down your thoughts or what the situation is like.

There are several parts to a script:

1. The first part is about the trauma. This might be about any of your triggers, whether it's someone telling you that you can't have what you want, being hit or abused, being rejected, a big disappointment, or another situation where your needs weren't met. It could also include other kinds of trauma, such as being in a car crash or experiencing a natural disaster. It could be a recollection from the past or a recent occurrence. It might even be something that happened many years ago, but that still comes up for you now and then.

2. The second part is about what you did to deal with your stress. For example, maybe you tried something that worked for a while, but then it became harder and harder to do. Maybe it didn't work the way you thought it would. Maybe you tried some things that almost worked but not quite, and now you don't know what else to do. Then write about the feelings that go with those ideas and thoughts.

* Remember, you're not just describing what happened. You're also writing about your feelings because that's what makes a script useful for dealing with stress.

3. The third part is about your reactions to the trauma and how those reactions made you feel. This is the heart of what the trauma did to you. It could be things like shame and guilt or feeling defective or bad about yourself. It might also be anxiety or depression, or even panic attacks or post-traumatic stress disorder (PTSD). If it negatively affects your life, then write about that as well.

4. The fourth part is about what helps you or makes a difference. That could be anything, but it should probably include things you didn't try before. For example, maybe you had problems trusting someone or asking for help in the past, but now you've learned how to do that, by trying a new method. Sometimes, it's just the idea of the thing itself that helps. But if you haven't tried those things before, it would be good to give them a try and see how they work for you.

After writing down all those parts and your feelings about them, read through what you wrote several times more. Some people write their scripts at least ten times before they start acting on the things in the script. Sometimes, writing the script is just a way to get started on something you normally wouldn't do. That's okay. Just do what makes sense for you.

You can find ways to change the script to make it more useful for you. You can also change parts of the script that don't work so well for you anymore. The idea is to make it so that you can feel better and deal with your life's stressors more healthily.

When you start doing the script, use it in a place where you won't be interrupted. You can do it under your bed or in a closet or somewhere that isn't visible to others. Use your script whenever you feel stressed, and then go about your normal life. The more often you use it, the fewer times you'll have to choose between dealing with stress and hiding from it.

Remember these things when using your script:

- Keep track of what goes through your mind while using the script. You might notice some good ideas and other things you can write down next time you use the script.

- Don't let the stress of using the script make you angry or upset. Just keep remembering what helps and what makes you feel better.

- Remember that your mind is amazing. When you use your script, it will help you understand how to handle stress better in the future. When you learn from a written plan, it's easier for you to remember than if you have to figure it out independently.

- Remember not to try too hard when using the script.

Allow the words to flow naturally.

- Remember to do what works for you. Use the script, but don't overdo it because that can worsen things.

Sometimes, writing a script for yourself makes a difference in your life. That's because scripts are meant to help you learn how to handle stress better in YOUR way. That might be something different from what other people do, and that's cool too. If you use your script with these things in mind and follow the steps above, you'll probably find that it works well for you.

Changing a Negative Thought Pattern into a Positive One

Many people have a habit of getting stuck on a negative thought pattern and then asking themselves questions like: What should I do? What am I going to do? Why does this keep happening to me? Those questions lead to other thoughts, such as "I'm stupid for doing this."

Once you recognize your habit for negative thinking, breaking the negative thought pattern will be much easier. You might not be able to change how other people feel or the things that happen around you, but you can change how you react to these challenging situations. There is no need to get upset about it.

Here are some ideas for changing negative thought patterns into positive ones:

- Sit quietly and think of something really good that happened recently. Imagine how you would feel if the same thing happened again in the future.

- Remember a time when you handled something well. Think about how you were feeling and what your actions were like.

- Think of what you've done so far to make yourself a better person. Try to identify at least one positive thing that you've been able to do.

- Realize that there is always something good that can happen even if things don't always work out the way you want them to.

- Try to think of at least one example of a time in the past when you made something work out well. Think about what you did and how your actions helped things work out in the end.

- Think about when someone helped you with something or showed you how to deal with something hard for you. Imagine you are looking into their eyes and ask yourself why they were able to do this for you.

- Think about something negative that has happened to you or someone close to you in the past. Find some good things about this incident. What positives can you take away from it?

- Think about the positive things that you are doing for others. We will never truly know how much of an impact we make on other people's lives.

- Remember how other people try to help you and how they do the best they can with what they have at hand. Not everything works out well, but it doesn't mean other people are stupid or mean.

Sometimes it feels really good to change a negative thought pattern into a positive one. When you do so, you start to feel much better about yourself, and you stop allowing negative thoughts to be a part of your life. Negative thoughts can cause stress, but when you transform them into positive ones, it's much easier for you to handle stressful situations. If a negative thought keeps coming back to you, try to change it into a positive one.

PART 4 - TRAUMA BONDING RECOVERY

CHAPTER 13: STRATEGIES TO STOP GASLIGHTING

Gaslighting is a significant component of trauma bonds and can cause the abused to doubt their abilities and experiences. When someone is gaslighted, they are led to believe that something they know to be true never happened at all. This manipulation can cause the abused to feel that their thoughts and feelings are invalid. Additionally, it can cause them to doubt their own perceptions, impairing their ability to think clearly, if at all. It causes victims to mistrust themselves, experts and authorities, and others. It can also cause them to doubt their sanity and experience feelings of isolation.

As a result of gaslighting and other manipulative tactics, some victims may begin to think that their abuser is the only person who knows what's really going on, and that no one else understands them or cares about their situation. This kind of emotional warfare can interfere with a victim's ability to receive help from others because they don't want anyone else questioning their thoughts or feelings too closely. An abusive partner may even convince the victim that they imagine their abuse and that no one else can see things the way they do. In addition, sometimes the victim will lose touch with reality and believe the abuser when they claim to be feeling something they've never felt before. This change in their state of mind can be especially hard on children or young adults who are still trying to develop healthy coping mechanisms for stress.

In other cases, gaslighting may take a more subtle form and make it difficult for a victim to recognize what's going on in their relationship. They might begin to not trust their thoughts or feelings about what is happening. For example, they might believe that the abuse is normal and that it's just a part of their relationship. Victims may convince themselves out of self-preservation that the abuse is their fault or not happening in the first place. Instead of trying to understand why their relationship is violent, they may convince themselves, "it's just a crazy thing we sometimes do," or even "things would be better if I were more careful." As a result, victims may struggle with feelings of self-blame, shame, and despair.

A victim must become empowered to stop gaslighting and other types of manipulative tactics. This can happen one step at a time by understanding how the abuser is manipulating them and finding ways to counteract those tactics. Part of doing this means learning to recognize what kind of abuse you are experiencing and getting help from friends and family who can provide support and validation for your feelings.

Putting it All into Perspective

The trauma bond can make it difficult for a victim to see the abuse for what it really is. Once the emotional, physical and verbal abuse begins, the trauma bond makes it hard for the victim to detach from their abuser and harder to forgive themselves. If you find yourself in this situation, you should seek help from friends, family, or professionals. This can help you heal and find peace with your situation and remember that you are not alone in your struggle. Realizing that you are not to blame for the abuse can be very healing at a time when thoughts of self-harm and suicide are common. Remember that you are not crazy, and people want to help you. People want to help because they love and support you. If you're not sure you should seek help, talk to those who care about you and ask for their guidance.

Taking Control of Your Life

While the past is unchangeable, you can reclaim control of your life and relationships in the future. This means recognizing what happened to you and finding ways to strengthen yourself going forward. This starts with asking for help from trusted friends, family, or professionals who want to help you heal to reach a healthy place in your life. If you are a victim of abuse, keep in mind that it is not your fault and seek help immediately before the abuse escalates. Understanding the abuse for what it is and taking control of your life one step at a time will go a long way towards helping you find peace, no matter what happens in the future.

Breaking the bonds of trauma can be the most challenging part of coping with abuse. It's critical to remember, however, that no one knows how you feel unless you express it. They can only see what happens for themselves, and they are not your judge and jury. Sharing your feelings about what happened will help you heal and understand the situation better.

Remember that you deserve to feel safe in your relationship and be free from violence. No matter what happened in the past, being abused was not your fault. This is why it is critical for you to reclaim control of your life by seeking assistance from those who care about you.

The Importance of Having no Contact with the Abuser

Once the exit plan has begun, the abuser will often start to do things to make the victim feel guilty for leaving. They might call, text, or visit the victim and tell them how they want them back because they love them and want to work things out. This is just a trick so that the victim won't feel comfortable moving forward with their life away from the abuse. For this reason, it is best if the victim has no contact with their abuser. Victims in coercive relationships must remember that their abusers will go to any lengths to reclaim them. Being left will make the abuser angry and lead to even more abuse.

Suppose, however, that the victim needs to stay in touch with them for certain reasons, perhaps because of shared custody of children. In that case, they can do so safely by asking a friend or family member for help or asking a professional to do it for them if they are not comfortable making contact themselves. If a victim must contact the abuser after an abusive situation, they should keep the relationship from becoming too comfortable or intimate. For example, if a victim regularly has contact with the abuser for extended periods, it can create an unhealthy situation for both parties.

Additionally, victims should have no contact with anyone the abuser knows, including their family and friends.

It is common for victims to feel guilty about leaving their abusers. They may feel like something is wrong with them for wanting to leave. Remember that experiencing abuse can be a normal state of life for victims, but the trauma they experienced is not their fault, and it shouldn't define their identity as a person.

Focus on Recovery

The biggest thing to remember is that you are not responsible for the abuse. You can't help who the abuser chooses to abuse. It's important to realize this and use it to your advantage to heal and move forward.

Victims of domestic violence do not have much control over their situation, so it is important to reach out for help and keep people close by who support you in your decision.

The victim should understand that any abuse they experience can be controlled by following the safety plan. Victims should stop blaming themselves and learn to define their self-worth as something other than what they have been told.

Survivors of domestic violence who have a support system in place tend to cope better than those who attempt to go it alone.

Victims must be kind to themselves by engaging in activities they enjoy and feel good about, such as going for a walk or pursuing a hobby or training that has personal significance for them. They should remember that they are worthy of respect and kindness.

Treatment can help victims learn how to manage their feelings and deal with situations more effectively so they can remain safe and healthy.

Victims of abuse have a wealth of resources at their disposal, and a supportive network can go a long way toward helping them cope. Getting involved in organizations that provide victims with the help they need, such as shelters or support groups, can make a huge difference in their coping ability. Victims should take control of their lives and take time to focus on themselves by engaging in activities that make them feel good about themselves and leave them feeling happy when they are finished.

Spend your time focusing on all the things you have accomplished rather than the trauma you experienced. Even if forgiving yourself or the abuser is difficult, this will make it easier for you to move forward with your life and find healthy peace.

Negative beliefs accumulate over time in many different ways, and they can be passed on from one generation to another. The victim's beliefs about themselves and their feelings about the abuse are often reflected in what they learned during their childhood. Hence, victims need to understand how abuse trauma may have affected them in their early years.

Children who grew up in abusive homes frequently exhibit inappropriate behavior as adults as a result of the abuse they endured as children. They may believe that they are not as valuable as others. They may also feel bad that they cannot live up to their parents' expectations and be afraid that they will be abused again if they make a mistake. Victims must learn to break these negative beliefs about themselves in order to move forward.

They should try to understand how their childhood experiences are affecting them. They should take responsibility for their actions and start believing that they can do anything or achieve anything they put their minds to. Victims should not give up on themselves because they can overcome the abuse and move forward with who they were meant to be.

CHAPTER 14: THE CHALLENGES OF TRAUMA BOND RECOVERY

The healing process itself can be traumatic, as in order to properly heal, the trauma must be relived. Suppose a victim is in the very early stages of recovery. They may feel depressed or anxious if they think about their past actions. They need to work on their feelings and get on a positive track of living a healthy and safe life.

A relationship in recovery needs positive reinforcement from both the participants. The partners must feel safe enough to leave their old ideas behind and move forward with a new mind-set.

If one person is recovering and their partner is not, they will have to live in a constant state of watching out for a potential attack. This can make the victim feel like they are on guard instead of living their lives, which will not help them recover. During this stage, the recovering partner may also feel angry at their abuser or themselves and continue to judge themselves harshly. All this judgment keeps them stuck and unable to realize that healing is possible. A victim has to be ready for recovery before they even start it. Otherwise, it can seem too much stress to handle, and backslide occurs.

When one partner is in recovery, they might feel that the other one is ignoring them or is being inconsiderate. The abuser may also stop taking care of the victim's needs financially, which can cause resentment. These factors will lead to recovery back-sliding and more trauma. When one partner keeps acting out, their actions will make the victim feel alone, which may deter them from believing that they can heal. This feeling can make it harder for victims to live healthily and free from their abusive relationship.

The partners must seek support from friends and family while in recovery. If they do not have support, both parties will feel alone and become more depressed or anxious. They can also feel scared and uncertain about the future, which will keep them stuck in an unhealthy relationship. The partners also need to stop blaming their partner for everything.

In recovery, the partners must work on the communication and trust between them. One partner might decide to talk to their abuser or become more confrontational. This may cause conflict in their relationship. If a partner is hurting because of their abusive partner's behaviors, they need to get away from them and get support from others who will help them heal from this trauma.

Victims may have a hard time taking care of themselves, especially if kids are involved. During recovery, the partners must work on their feelings together to create a healthy environment for themselves and their kids. If one partner does not cooperate in recovery, the other should try to take care of themselves with support from a loved one.

The partners can only get free if both people agree to let go of old behavior and change their ways. One partner may be triggered by something they saw when they were with the other person, making them act out against them instead of healing in a safe environment. When a partner acts out, the other person should stand up for themselves and stop accepting blame for everything.

When victims are in recovery, their abusive partner may keep trying to make them feel like they are not good enough. This complicates the victim's ability to recognize that the abuse is abnormal and must be stopped. If one partner continues to be abusive, he will cause the other person not only physical harm but also emotional. The abuser also keeps his partner from getting help or healing from trauma. The abuser needs to stop feeling so entitled and abusing the victim.

When one partner believes their partner loves them, they will often abuse them more. The abuser keeps the victim from getting free because he does not want to lose his object of love. This is a root cause of domestic violence and can keep partners stuck in their unhealthy relationship for a very long time. The abusive partner may also start acting crazy to prevent the victim from getting help or healing from this abuse.

If a victim is in recovery, they may start to feel afraid of their partner, their situation, and everyone around them. This may cause the victim to feel trapped and as though they have no choice but to stay in the relationship.

When a victim tries to get free from their abuser, they need support from others who will understand how they feel and help them heal from this trauma. If either partner starts harassing or stalking the other one, this behavior can also stop them from getting help or healing from domestic violence abuse.

Dealing with Loneliness and Your Insecurities

While leaving an abusive relationship can be liberating and empowering, it can also cause you to feel lonely, sad, and depressed. This is common when moving away from an abuser, especially if the you were in the habit of seeking out their attention and loving them. Some people react to this by becoming more dysfunctional to cope; others want help before they're pushed further into their darkness. There are, however, resources available for those who require assistance or who are unsure of where to turn or what they can do.

Loneliness, hurt, and emptiness will come on different days, weeks, and months. You may feel this way even when you are with other people. The abuser can no longer be there to share your days with you or fill the void inside you. Even if they've tried to make you feel like it's your fault that they hurt you or that you're a bad person for wanting to leave them, these negative feelings are still real. You might have even thought about their pain and how much scarier their life could have been if things had turned out differently for the two of you.

You may wonder: "What has brought me here? What is the point of my life if I am unable to spend it with the person I love?" Your mind will tell you things like: "You're no good. You deserve this. You don't deserve happiness." Or "They will forget you. You aren't worth it." Or "You made them do this to you. You should have never gotten involved with them in the first place." These thoughts might make you feel hopeless or powerless, and as if there is nothing that you can do to end these horrible thoughts. The hardest part of leaving an abusive relationship is blaming yourself for somehow making it so bad for others that they'd want to hurt and control you. You may be so convinced that you're the reason for their behavior and pain, sometimes it can even seem like nobody else exists. It's not that you have to know why this relationship went wrong. You don't have to know the reason, but you need to understand that there are people who care about you and want to help you.

Some people will react by trying to control every aspect of their life, or making big decisions such as changing jobs, changing their name and social security number, moving out of town, or even just locking themselves in a room until they stop feeling so lonely. The effects of depression also make some people more vulnerable.

Many people think that they have no other way out than clinging to what they have left in this relationship. They may feel that they can't stand on their own two feet and that abandoning the abuser is more difficult than what they're prepared to do. They might also be afraid of being alone and forget how strong they are. Others may fear becoming homeless if they attempt to move out.

Here are some strategies for overcoming your loneliness and insecurities:

Write down any negative thoughts so you can look back over them and see how they affect you.

1

____

2

____

3

____

4

____

5

____

6

____

7

____

8

____

- Talk to someone about any difficult experiences or feelings that may be cluttering your mind. Seek assistance from a therapist or a friend who will listen to you without passing judgment.

- Remember that it takes courage to set the old patterns

aside and reach for the new.

- Ask yourself how you'd like to feel or act and do something that will help you achieve your goals.

- Understand that this is a time to be yourself, not anyone else.

- Accept yourself and be willing to forgive. Forgiving others will help you release them so you can move on and live your life.

- If there are any feelings of fear or guilt, just acknowledge them, but don't judge them. Let them flow through you so they don't consume you.

- Remember that overcoming these obstacles is the best way to overcome sadness for good.

- Remind yourself that you deserve to be happy and don't let anyone tell you otherwise.

- Seek counseling or therapy, if needed.

Many people do not know that resources are available for them outside of their friends and family members. Often, the abuser will discourage the victim from going to shelters, hospitals, and police stations because they could see them as a threat to their survival. Some abusers may even lie and tell the victim that the authorities will take away their children. If you require help:

- Go to a hospital or police station in your area. Find out whether they have a program for victims of domestic abuse or what options are available to you.

- Find a domestic violence shelter.

- Find a rape crisis center if you have been raped.

- Make a list of people you can call in an emergency.

- At all times, ensure that your family and friends know how to contact you. Have a cell phone or borrow one if necessary.

- If the abuser has threatened to harm you or someone else, report them to the police, especially if they are already harming or threatening other people around them.

- Remove guns, drugs, or weapons from the home, as well as any medications that could be harmful to yourself or others.

- Keep critical legal and financial documents in a secure location to ensure they are accessible in the event of a move.

- Find out about community services that can help you with temporary housing, food, and clothing.

A person in an abusive relationship may feel that they have lost their dignity because their world has been turned upside down, and they don't know how to deal with their feelings of shame. They might also feel embarrassed because of what they've allowed other people to do to them. They might believe that they're no longer a good person because they've been controlled and abused in the past.

The victim might feel like a victim of their own emotions or thoughts because of how helpless they may feel when someone hurts them. They might also feel like a bad person for letting it happen, not having the courage to end it, or thinking about moving on without dealing with the situation properly.

Victims may also feel embarrassed or guilty about coming forward. Additionally, they might feel embarrassed because they can't do more to end what's happening.

Feeling anxious during an abusive relationship is normal and natural. However, the longer abuse lasts, the tenser you may feel. You might also have symptoms of depression like crying more often or losing interest in things that used to make you happy. Depression can also make people feel more anxious in general and hopeless about any change in a positive direction.

You might experience physical symptoms of anxiety, like a tight stomach, tension headaches, vision problems, dizziness, or any combination of these.

If you're in an abusive situation and a friend or family member tries to tell you how to end it, listen to them but don't take what they say as absolute truth. Your situation is highly personal and may require a different solution.

. With this in mind, it's critical to remember that there is always someone who can assist you. The first step towards recovery requires creating a plan for yourself and your future. Look for counseling services at local hospitals or domestic abuse shelters in your area.

Getting Back on Track and Understanding Your Life Purpose

The road to recovery is not easy, but it is very rewarding. Your journey begins within you.

To begin this long process, it is helpful to ask yourself a few questions:

- What type of relationship do I want in the future?

- What are my strongest qualities?

- Who am I without my abuser (or abusers)?

- What have I learned from the past?

- How can I use this knowledge to my advantage?

Having healthy self-esteem while going through any situation can help you overcome obstacles. Remember always to be confident in yourself and keep your mind strong. Empowering yourself can help with a positive attitude and self-esteem. Remember that the road to recovery is not fast and may take time, but it is worth it. Remember that many survivors initially had no idea how to escape their situations. Empower yourself, be patient, and believe in yourself. You can overcome this obstacle with the assistance of professionals and local organizations that offer domestic abuse victim support groups.

People who are abused often feel confused about what they need or deserve, and never have the strength or determination to leave the situation. They often lose themselves in this process, making it more difficult for them to escape their situation.

Leaving an abusive relationship will take courage and strength, but it is possible.

CHAPTER 15: BUILDING HEALTHY RELATIONSHIPS

After your recovery, you have doubts about starting a new relationship. It is necessary to remember that it will take some time for you to regain trust in others, and yourself.

Lack of trust comes from a feeling of being hurt. Lack of trust needs to be overcome through honest and open communication, self-forgiveness, and forgiveness of your ex-partner. You will need to work on relationship skills in order to rebuild trust. You may want to take a relationship skills class or read books about healthy relationships, such as *Daring Greatly* by Brenc Brown, who writes about the importance of vulnerability in a relationship.

Confronting fears and taking risks are necessary to build self-trust. One aspect of building trust is examining your values and beliefs and looking at your actions through the lens of these values.

Taking risks, such as speaking honestly and directly, is like stepping into the dark end of a tunnel. You will have to perform in that situation to find out who you are. Revealing things about yourself you may have always tried to hide is necessary for growing as an individual and continuing on the journey toward self-trust. Having a partner who understands your fears, has taken risks, and has learned from their mistakes will help you accept yourself, even with your mistakes.

Another aspect of self-trust is being able to forgive yourself for your mistakes and be willing to let go of any history you may have with a former partner. The only way to gain trust in yourself and others is through forgiveness. The ability to forgive, or rather the willingness to forgive, is the first step in healing. Once someone has forgiven themselves, it prepares them for moving forward in their lives.

Many people say they never realized how much they wanted forgiveness until they were finally ready to forgive themselves. By forgiving ourselves and others, we can love again.

We are more likely to forgive others when we have forgiven ourselves for our mistakes.

Conflict is an inevitable part of life. The key to healing from an abusive relationship involves the ability to respond assertively when one's boundaries or values are crossed. It is important to have assertive communication skills, along with the willingness to stand up for yourself and your values, even if it means ending the relationship. This can be difficult, as it may feel small-minded or immature. Additionally, your emotions may be triggered by the situation.

Building a New Relationship

A partner who is aware of their needs and limits, and who has healthy boundaries for self and others, understands how to set boundaries in a relationship. This includes the willingness to end a relationship if the other person does not respect those boundaries. A healthy relationship will also be marked by emotional intimacy and vulnerability, which can be difficult to develop after a traumatic relationship.

It is important to examine your past experiences with relationships known as attachment injuries. These are common in both women and men, but how their parents and caregivers treat them may determine whether they seek help to resolve these issues. Also, society encourages women to be nurturing and men to be tough. Men are more likely to handle problems with alcohol or drugs and not seek counseling. Women may feel the need to please others or pretend nothing is wrong. Additionally, women are more likely than men to have a broader definition of what constitutes abuse in a relationship.

It is essential to understand your needs and values thoroughly before setting boundaries in a new relationship. Although it will not be easy, an honest discussion with yourself and your potential partner is necessary for success. Your true needs must be understood by both partners so you can develop real trust and an intimate connection.

When a boundary violation occurs, you must stand up for yourself and let the other person know how you feel. Do not let yourself be used or verbally abused. It takes courage to stand up to someone who has wronged you.

The ultimate goal of learning emotional self-trust and boundary setting is to become a mature adult who can form healthy relationships. Remember that you deserve better than what you have experienced, and you will find it one day if you dare to pursue it.

Decide When You Are Ready to be in a Relationship

If you are ready to be in a relationship, you should take the necessary steps to ensure that your new partner understands your needs and boundaries and is willing to meet them. You'll want to discuss this new relationship with a friend or family member. An impartial friend who will not interfere may be a good choice.

Once again, it is important to set realistic expectations. If possible, both partners should write down what they expect from the relationship, including how long they would like the relationship to last.

It would be beneficial if you avoided making unrealistic promises regarding time, distance, or children unless you require them for your own reasons. For example, if you want to be with your partner, but they live in another state and do not want to move, you are setting yourself up for disappointment.

As you talk about "what ifs," keep in mind that both of you should be able to agree on what happens if the relationship ends. You may need an exit plan in case something bad happens. If it involves children or financial issues, get some help from friends who have been through the process so that you do not make the same mistakes again.

It would help to discuss how your past experiences may affect the relationship. The person you are dating may have a history of abuse, but this is not an excuse for treating you poorly.

You also need to decide what your needs are and how important they are to you—and be sure to stick to them.

Decide what you need to do for yourself and make your own decisions. If someone does not want to accept your boundaries and limits, this is a clear sign that the relationship will not work. It may be a good idea to talk about your safety with a trusted friend or family member in case of emergencies.

Bear in mind that you have the right to feel secure in your environment, and no one has the authority to violate that boundary.

Emotional Strength is Achieved by Sticking to Your Boundaries

Emotional strength is a core component of self-trust and healthy boundaries. It involves the ability to stand up for yourself and speak the truth about what you feel so that others get the message that you have had enough.

As with physical strength, emotional strength takes time and training. It involves not giving anyone permission to touch your body inappropriately, or force you into any sexual activity.

You alone can determine when it is acceptable for someone to care for you and when it is not. Your boundaries should never be violated by anyone who does not have your permission to touch you in any way.

You must be able to set your boundaries and stick to them. You will not progress very far if you do not understand or are unable to adhere to your boundaries.

Your emotional strength also gives you the ability to stand up for yourself if someone tries to hurt you or use abusive behaviors against you. You may be afraid of their anger, but this does not mean that they have any right to treat you badly or make threats about harming themselves if you do not give in to their demands. Tell them in a clear and firm voice that they can take care of themselves and stop trying to get you to do it. You need to know your limits and stick to them, regardless of how hard things get or what it costs you.

Emotional strength does not come overnight, but it is possible if you are willing to take the steps needed for change. The more time and effort that goes into setting boundaries and sticking with them, the easier it will be in the long run.

Your emotional strength is a powerful tool that can help you live a healthy and safe life. Once you have it, people will know that you mean business, and they need to respect you. You will also be able to set boundaries in your relationships so that it functions as it should.

Have a Fulfilling, Loving Relationship, Regardless of Your History

Regardless of your relationship history, you are able to have a satisfying, healthy relationship.

Your past experiences do not affect your ability to build a healthy and lasting relationship with the right person.

You need the emotional strength to "get over" the abuse, and not let it affect how you choose to relate in the future. It would be beneficial if you possessed the confidence to select someone who adheres to your rules and respects your boundaries. It would help if you also had the self-esteem to be happy and confident in yourself, regardless of what others think about you.

A healthy relationship involves two people who are committed to respecting each other. If either of you compromises your boundaries and attempts to control or dominate the other, this is not a healthy relationship. A person who tries to control you or punish you should take a step back and make some changes.

This is not about someone needing to change for you to be happy. It's about both people committing themselves to each other and respecting each other's limits as well as their need for love, support, and respect.

If you have trouble setting limits, it will help if you seek therapy to learn what is important in life and how to get out of un-fulfilling relationships that do not add anything good to your life. You can also seek therapy if you are trying to build up your emotional and spiritual strength.

It would help if you had the emotional strength to protect yourself from anyone who does not respect your boundaries or who tries to control you in any way.

You need to tell someone who is doing this that they are acting like a bully and that you will no longer stand for them violating your boundaries and trying to control you.

It also helps if you have self-confidence and the self-esteem necessary to build a healthy relationship. If one of you in the relationship lacks these, it will be much harder for that relationship to work out successfully.

Think about your needs and your wants in a relationship. You should get your needs met and have somebody who cares about you, just like you care about them.

You will have gone a long way towards gaining the emotional strength you need for healthy relationships if you can leave unhealthy relationships behind when they do not work out. If you are still with someone who is trying to control or abuse you, that person is abusing their control of the relationship and ignoring your boundaries. If they do not get the help they need to change, they may eventually resort to threats or violence in an attempt to convince you that it is in your best interest to stay with them. It is not.

If you have finally had enough, you will need emotional strength to let them go and move on with your life. You need to know your limits, stick to them, and treat yourself with compassion.

It will help if you also know when it is time to leave a relationship that is not working out, and that will lead you down a path of ongoing hurt, depression, or anxiety.

You should be able to leave someone who does not respect your boundaries for their emotional well-being and yours.

How to approach the relationship in a way that works

You will have more success in your relationships if you remember some basic rules:

- This is not about your past. It is about who you are and what happens from this point forward.

- This is not about doing things for other people but rather doing things for both of you. If someone does not do things for you, it simply means that they are selfish and neglectful.

- This is not about playing games but about being honest and open with each other.

- This is not about expecting someone to change for you. It's about focusing on each other's needs and wants rather than on what others want from you.

- This is not about giving someone more than they deserve, but rather respecting your boundaries while accepting that they are the only ones who can decide what they have to give or receive from you. Selfishness, lack of respect, and dismissive behavior are evidence that this person does not understand their own needs and wants.

- This is not a power trip where one person dictates your every move or tells you how to act, but rather about independent decision making and mutual respect of each other's boundaries.

- This is not about what someone else deserves, but rather about what you want and need. You are entitled to want or need support, love, and respect.

- This is a partnership in which two people have their own needs and wants. If either one of them does not understand their feelings or needs, they should take steps to figure this out.

- This is not about winning, but rather knowing that you can be yourself while allowing the other person to do the same in return.

- This is not about always having to say sorry for things that were not your fault, but rather knowing when you have done something wrong or crossed a boundary, and being able to apologize when appropriate.

- This is not a mistake where things will be fine in a few hours, but rather an honest conversation where both of you can learn that your actions caused an emotional upheaval in the other person.

- This is not about someone taking advantage of you but rather about letting them know when they have taken things too far and violated your boundaries.

- This is not about someone accepting or rejecting you but rather them knowing how you feel and whether or not your needs are being met.

- This is not about expecting others to do something for you, but rather asking them if they are willing to do things you need.

- This is not just a label or a word, but rather a real commitment to both of your needs, wants, and feelings.

- This is not a parent or authority figure but rather a real and loving adult relationship.

-

This is not about money, but rather knowing how to communicate about each other's financial needs. Then it's about doing what you can to help with this, whether that means seeking out professional advice or looking for ways to find common ground between your needs and theirs.

- This is not about having superpowers, but rather about being willing to ask for support from those who can provide it and being able to directly tell the people in your life what you need from them.

- This is not about someone always fulfilling your needs, but rather about making sure that you are also doing things for them.

- This is not about controlling people, but rather about being able to have distance from them when you need it.

- This is not about getting away from something that causes you to feel bad, but rather understanding how to work out what caused this problem so that the negative feelings do not come back again.

- This is not about dwelling in the past but rather about looking positively towards the future together.

- This is not about finding a scapegoat but rather learning how to deal with your emotions so that you can start getting what you want in life.

- This is not a competition, but rather a way of understanding how people work together by respecting their differences.

- This is about accepting that you are both in this relationship, and it's up to you two together to make things work.

If you want someone who understands their own needs and wants as well as yours, then let them know that this is what they will get if they are with you.

If you are in a relationship that does not work for you, it is time to change things. You will need to tell this person how you feel and let them know that you need something other than what they offer.

You have a right to have your needs met, and if this person will not meet them for you, then it is time to find someone who will. The next step is determining what those needs are, establishing boundaries for yourself, and recognizing when someone else has crossed those boundaries.

CHAPTER 16: THE POWER OF DEVELOPING INTERPERSONAL CONNECTIONS

Many people today are afraid of being alone and afraid they will miss out on the "love" they think they have been missing. However, it is important to also focus on other areas of your life. You might want to focus on your job, family, and friends or a hobby that you love doing.

We all want to fit in somewhere or feel like we belong with someone. The fact is we all have different personalities and do things differently than others to make life work for us. Nonetheless, you are always going to need people in your life. You can't live without relationships, but you can control the quality of your relationships.

After you have been abused, I know it's hard to trust a new person. However, it would be best to make an effort because you never know where it may lead. You may find that this person is the one who can help you get on your feet and encourage you to become a better person. You may notice that this person has a positive attitude towards life and enjoys being with people. If you like what you see after spending some time getting to know each other, then maybe it's time for the two of you to start dating or becoming friends.

Sometimes you may feel lonely and think that you need a date or someone to be with in order to truly feel loved or to fill up the void in your life. The fact is that we often need others around us in our lives to feel special and loved. But if you feel that someone does not love you, it's best not to ignore the signs. You also want to make sure that people are who they say they are so you can make an informed decision about whether or not it would be a good idea for the two of you to start dating.

You must exercise caution regarding who you associate with and the type of situation in which you find yourself. Some people will marry simply because they are lonely and want someone to be around. But you need is someone who cares about you, supports you, and believes in your goals and dreams.

If there's someone in your life who loves you, they'll listen to your frustrations and try to help you resolve them. They'll want to be with you when things are going well and when they aren't. They won't give up on you just because the going gets tough. They will work together with you, support you, and love you unconditionally, no matter what happens in your life or the world around them.

A person who cares about someone is willing to make sacrifices for them. They will care about your needs and sometimes even put their own needs aside for you. They're there for you even when things go wrong in your life. You can rely on them in the long run, regardless of what happens on a daily basis.

Hopefully, you now understand what it means to be in a relationship with someone who cares about you and how this kind of person can help change your life for the better. To someone who cares about you, you're special and will always maintain a place in their lives. Don't lose sight of that, and don't let anyone make you feel less than important because when someone loves you, it's unconditional.

CONCLUSION

Trauma bonds keep us trapped in this unhealthy relationship and make it difficult or impossible to escape. However, once we realize what's happening and how these bonds manifest, we can take appropriate measures to break them before they become more debilitating or lethal.

The term "trauma bond" is used to describe an unhealthy bond that forms when trauma is experienced by one person at the hands of another. This reaction can be positive or negative, depending on how it manifests. Either way, it keeps both people in the same disturbing situation regardless of how gently or firmly they try to break free from it.

Trauma bonds are not loving or abusive; rather, they are the attachment that forms as a result of trauma in one person. We need to understand that a trauma bond isn't a problem in and of itself, but it can be if it keeps us stuck in a cycle of abuse or puts us in danger. They can form between two people who love each other or between one individual suffering from trauma and someone trying to help them heal.

This book is not meant to help victims better understand the different types of abuse, how they affect victims in different ways, and how it can be prevented or stopped. Victims of abuse need to realize that they are the only ones who have the power to stop the abuse.

There is no justification for anyone to harm another person, regardless of what they did or said. Someone who truly loves you won't ever deliberately hurt you; they will stand by your side and help you heal until you're able to overcome the challenges you face. An abusive partner won't do any of these things; instead, they will blame their actions on you and insist that their behavior is your fault for reasons that have nothing to do with the situation.

An abusive partner will always be emotionally unavailable and emotionally volatile, if not outright abusive. The abused will often blame themselves for the abuse they suffered or even agree with their abuser that they deserve their treatment. If your partner is being hurtful and hateful, it's not your responsibility to change how they feel — you can only control how you react to what they say or do and ensure the way you react is based on something rational and not fear or anger. This doesn't mean that you can't get upset – no one should be expected to put up with abuse – but it's always important to remember that your partner can only change if they want to.

Once you realize that your partner is an abusive person, getting away from them is the best option because it will allow you to heal and recover from the trauma. If your partner is a victim of abuse themselves, they may not rationally understand what's happening; this will make things worse for them instead of better, so it's up to you to get them some help. If your partner is a victim of abuse and you leave them, they may become suicidal, which is why it's necessary to check in with them regularly until they get some help. For example, if you know that your partner is feeling suicidal or depressed, talk to them as if nothing had happened and let them know they can come back home when they feel better.

Your past is important, but it should not ruin your future. You may have experienced abusive relationships as a child or teen, but this does not mean you will automatically continue to be abused in your adult relationships. You do not have to tolerate abuse just because you have been abused in the past.

This does not mean that you have to forgive your abuser or give them an excuse for their behavior. It means, however, that you are free to live in ways that allow you the safety and respect you deserve.

You have the right to have a loving, respectful relationship with someone who respects your boundaries and limits. You have earned the right to be treated equally in a happy and healthy relationship.

You might want to share your experience with an online or in-person support group, but remember that you are the only person who can decide what is best for you. The decision is yours, and no one else can make it for you. You may feel better if you find support from others who understand what it feels like to be abused, but whatever works for you is all right.

Feelings of shame about being abused will begin to fade away as you begin setting boundaries and protecting yourself from abuse in any form. Then you can begin to feel respect for yourself and increased self-worth.

It would be beneficial if you also learned to distinguish between healthy and unhealthy relationships in order to make more informed choices in the future. You might also think about whether you are ready to take on another person's past and whether or not they are ready to take on yours.

It may be appropriate to wait until you work through your past issues, to begin a new relationship, but that is up to you. Whatever you decide, set your boundaries and chart a course for your future relationship.

If needed, see a therapist who has experience working with abused people and learn how to move forward without sacrificing yourself through feelings of worthlessness or victim's guilt.

Set healthy boundaries, don't let anyone violate them. If your partner ignores these boundaries, gently insist that they respect your boundaries and let them know that you won't tolerate whatever they are doing anymore. Respect yourself, respect your body, respect your personal space and call out unwanted behavior if it starts happening. If you are with someone who is abusing you, get some professional help; it may be necessary to get out of their life for good.

Respect yourself and work to make yourself a better person so you don't attract those who abuse you in the future. Forgiving your abuser can be good for you, but making excuses for abuse is never good.

Abuse is always wrong. If someone wants to hurt you or use you, walk away because someone worth having will love and respect you enough to show it.

People who truly love and care about their partner will not try to justify or conceal abuse; they will instead respect themselves and the person they love enough not to cause them unnecessary harm.

Understanding that your partner's abusive behaviors are not "normal" may help you avoid excuses and rationalizations for the abuse. It never helps to make up excuses for their behavior, and it doesn't help to excuse the behavior by saying, "It's okay; he's just stressed out."

If someone expects you to put up with abuse, remember that you don't owe them anything. No one has a right to hurt you or treat you badly.

www.ingramcontent.com/pod-product-compliance
Lightning Source LLC
Chambersburg PA
CBHW050340160726
48002CB00001B/396